No........... E306014

AVON COUNTY
LIBRARY

D0294891

Farmhouses in the English Landscape

By the same author

Epping Forest: Its Literary and Historical Association
The English Country Parson
Essex Heyday
Essex Worthies
Worthy Dr Fuller
Audley End
Suffolk
Thames Estuary
English Spas
English Fairs and Markets
In the Steps of Charles Dickens
Understanding English Place-Names
Understanding English Surnames
Local Styles of the English Parish Church
The Old Roads of England
Portrait of Epping Forest

Farmhouses in the
English Landscape

SIR WILLIAM ADDISON

E306C14

CLASS No.	728.67
ALLOC.	AA / HJ.
AVON COUNTY LIBRARY	

ROBERT HALE · LONDON

© Sir William Addison 1986
First published in Great Britain 1986

Robert Hale Limited
Clerkenwell House
Clerkenwell Green
London EC1R 0HT

British Library Cataloguing in Publication Data

Addison, Sir William
  Farmhouses in the English landscape.
  1. Farmhouses — England   2. Architecture,
  Domestic — England
  I. Title
  728'.76'0942

ISBN 0-7090-2813-X

Photoset in Ehrhardt by
Derek Doyle & Associates, Mold, Clwyd
Printed in Great Britain by
St Edmundsbury Press Ltd, Bury St Edmunds, Suffolk
Bound by Woolnough Bookbinders Ltd

Contents

List of Illustrations

Line Illustrations by Joan Bill

Photographs

Between pages 48 and 49

Between pages 80 and 81

9

Photograph Credits

G.I. Sherren: 1-29, 31, 32, 36-57; Olive May: 8, 9, 33, 34, 35; Donald Jarvis Collection: 30; Derek G. Widdicombe: 58, 59

A Note of Thanks

My sincere thanks are due to all those owners and occupiers who very generously permitted me to enter their property to help illustrate this book. I hasten to add, however, that the majority of farms depicted herein are not open to the general public and readers are therefore asked to respect the privacy of others. I also wish to thank my driver for going safely round the corners and not round the bend.

Ian Sherren

Soames Forsyth visits the home of his ancestors and muses on their way of life:

It had been the old England, when they lived down here – the England of pack-horses and very little smoke, of peat and wood fires ... There'd be the church and your bible, he supposed, and the market some miles away, and you'd work and eat and sleep and breathe the air and drink your cider and embrace your wife and watch your children from June to June; and a good thing too! What more did you do now that brought you any satisfaction? 'Change, it's all on the surface,' thought Soames; 'the roots are the same. You can't get beyond them – try as you will!'

John Galsworthy, *Swan Song*

Introduction

On reflection I think this book must be a belated attempt to answer a question put to me more than forty years ago while taking a party of tourists round the English Lake District. When I casually told them the height of Bow Fell, a visitor from the Himalayas came up to me and said: 'Why do you say how high your hills are? 2,950 feet is not very high. I live at an altitude of 30,000 feet. Why do you not say that they are so romantic because they are dotted over with the little homes of your people?' We glory – and rightly – in our churches, castles and so on, and say little about the workaday buildings. Yet to this visitor from the Himalayas, surveying the Lakeland scene with eyes undimmed by familiarity, the Englishness of the landscape was in its farmhouses. And so it is everywhere. Rural England is the land the farmers made, and in every parish mellow old farmhouses, many of which were originally manor houses, reflect the true character of English country life.

The best were built in stages from Tudor and Stuart times onward, often retaining medieval timbers at the core, but they are too individualized to be classified in the precise periods we use for describing churches. So I have concentrated on a few regions in which local styles are exceptionally clear-cut, describing the architecture and use of local materials peculiar to them, the life traditionally lived in them, and all the things that country folk set most store on, particularly the food they cooked, in the sound belief that the proof of the pudding is in the eating. This is not a book for dieticians!

The story is a long one. To understand even present-day farmhouses it is necessary to know that since Roman times farmhouses have evolved from the same basic styles as churches, Celtic and Roman. Excavations of villa sites have shown that the smaller Roman farmhouses anticipated the Tudor, with central hall flanked by wings, and the larger the Georgian, with farm buildings grouped round a court, or foldyard, at the rear. At the end of the Occupation five out of every six villas in the South of England were farmed by Roman-British, who may be regarded as our first yeoman-farmers in the sense of being countrymen cultivating small, independent estates.

The way of life they established was continued by the Anglo-Saxons, who integrated well into the Roman-British way of life since many had experienced it elsewhere. What must seem strange is that until recently we knew so little about the houses they lived in. However, work done on Saxon village sites (such as those at Mucking on the Essex bank of the Thames, West Stow, north-west of Bury St Edmunds in Suffolk, Chalton in the Hampshire Downs, and Catholme on the River Trent) testifies to the continued simplicity of Saxon farm life in single buildings fifteen to eighteen feet wide, thirty to forty feet long, with cross passages rudely partitioned off between opposing doors midway along them. The word 'threshold' may be thought to suggest, *pace* the philologists, strong evidence that these cross passages, with the wind blowing through them, were used as threshing floors. In broad terms, the Saxons settled the lowlands, the Celts the hills, and racial as well as agrarian factors determined the differences in farming practices and consequently of farmhouse styles. The longhouse, with stock and family under one roof, has continued to be the commonest farmhouse style in hill country, for reasons that will be seen when we look at Cumbria and the Pennine dales. In the lowlands of the eastern corn belt it had been abandoned by the end of the sixteenth-century – largely as a result of much greater versatility in farming becoming possible with the early break-up of the medieval system of communal farming.

In all parts of England the first farmhouses were in groups for mutual protection, situated near streams for water and woodland from which timber could be taken for building. Incidentally, although we use the word 'farmhouse' for all periods, it does not appear in local records until 1598. In the Midlands especially, these village farmhouses were converted into short rows of labourers' cottages in the eighteenth-century, when new farmhouses were being built on enclosed land for letting to a new race of tenant farmers. Now, two centuries later, hundreds of these down-graded village farmhouses are being restored into pleasant houses of character for retired couples or younger people who prefer to live in the country and travel to work. Their occupation so long by tenants who lacked the means to modernize them has preserved their old features and made them admirable for study of the early form of timber-framed buildings, with a one-roomed aisled hall in which the farmer, his family and servants lived the whole of their indoor lives, sleeping together on mats or straw pallets under a coarse coverlet of shaggy material called dagswain, with a log for a pillow. If the farmer had prospered, he might have acquired the comfort of a straw mattress for himself and his wife, with a bag of chaff for their heads if the fleas were not too vexatious.

The fires in these medieval halls were either in the middle of the floor or against a screen called a reredos. On such hearths 'greasy Joan' would 'keel the pot' while the smoke curled upward to escape through a louvre in the thatch, or a gablet at the end of the hipped roof, until chimneys were introduced. These gablets, which were small openings in the form of inverted Vs, can still be seen as openings for ventilation in the roofs of old barns.

Inserting an upper floor into these lofty halls was out of the question. To escape from the smoke the first refinement was either to screen off part of the hall or to build a chamber onto one end of it for the private use of the farmer and his family. This development can often be recognized by one side of the door in an old farmhouse having more windows than the other. That some of these extensions were made in the fourteenth-century, and also that they were unpopular with the rest of the household, is shown in a passage in *The Vision of Piers Plowman*:

> Woe is the hall in all times and seasons
> Where neither lord nor lady likes to linger.
> Now each rich man has a rule to eat in secret,
> In a private parlour, for poor folks comfort,
> In a chamber with a chimney, perhaps, and leave the chief assembly
> Which was made for man to have meat and meals in:
> And all to spare to spend what another will spend afterwards.*

*Passus X, lines 98-104

As Langland was writing in the West Midlands, this early reference to a chimney is interesting – as also the use of the word 'parlour', which at that time could have meant bedroom or chamber.

The word for parlour or chamber that came into use at the next stage of development was 'solar'. Having achieved the amenity of a private room comparatively free from smoke at the end of the hall, the obvious thing to do was to insert balks, or beams, at ceiling level on which wool could be stored after a shearing. No doubt balks already existed in barns. The storage space over a cowhouse built into a barn in the North of England is still called 'the balks'. But a more ambitious purpose was conceived for the farmhouse once chimneys had been introduced into halls. A private apartment could be installed on the joists. When this was done, it was called a solar in the South of England, from the French *soler*, to continue, a word which sounded superior to parlour or chamber, to say nothing of balks, yet in fact the word was derived from the French *solive*, which merely meant floor joist!

The fifteenth century brought a major development to the timber-framed rectangular hall-house. In the South-east this took the form of wings, which in the sixteenth century were often jettied out to provide a more commodious private room than the one below it for the farmer and his wife. The dimensions of these wings can provide valuable clues to the prosperity of local farm life. This will be seen when we compare the difference between extensions to timber-framed farmhouses in the neighbouring counties of Essex and Kent during the Tudor and Stuart periods. For introductory purposes it is sufficient to mention that in looking at old farmhouses of this type two features should be noted. The first is whether the roof line follows an erratic course. Few early roofs had straight roof timbers. The second is whether the wings are symmetrical, which may show whether they were built at different times. It is necessary to say 'may' instead of 'will' because symmetry could have been introduced later. Timber-framing is far more tractable than stone for adaptation. On entering such a house, if one wing is found to have an inferior staircase, we may assume that this part of the house was originally for the use of family servants or retainers, which is what wings were built for by the Romans thirteen hundred years earlier.

18

Expansion backwards came with the addition of a lean-to behind the hall. This was called an outshut and usually had two rooms: a buttery for the storage of butts of ale – not butter – and a pantry for the storage of bread. This would contain a dough-trough like the one in the church at Alfriston in Sussex. Extension in breadth was done in this way because it provided double-room depth on the ground floor at minimum cost. A roof was provided for the outshut by extending the existing roof in 'catslide' fashion. To have taken the next step of making the whole of the farmhouse two rooms deep would then have been beyond the means of most owners. It would have required tie-beams and rafters heavier than the existing walls would bear without inserting costly intermediate posts.

There were, of course, exceptions. In Kent, the county well ahead of others in timber-framed building, a local builder actually contracted in 1500 to erect a house of two storeys throughout at Cranbrook,* and the dating of old timber buildings generally has had to be revised since radio-carbon analysis was introduced. This may not be sufficiently precise for individual cases, but multiple sampling from the same timber may allow the span of variation to be considerably reduced from present assessments. We have also had the advantage recently of Cecil Hewett's system of dating from the style of joints used to frame timbers together, which in important buildings can often be confirmed from official records. Local fashions have also played their part. In some parts of England there was a tendency for the size of the hall to decrease, with the prospect of other rooms being added laterally at a later date.

Cellars came late in ordinary farmhouses, although in the fourteenth-century hall-house 'Old Soar' at Plaxtol in Kent, which is attached to an eighteenth-century farmhouse and is now in the safe keeping of the National Trust, there is a barrel-vaulted cellar with access to the hall by a stone newel-stair from the farm kitchen. But 'Old Soar' cannot be submitted as a representative farmhouse. In a tower on the solar floor there is a small chapel or oratory, and balancing it architecturally is a small room in another tower adjoining the main chamber, containing sanitary facilities drained

*Kent Record Office: Agreement of 9 March, 15 Henry VII.

through an arch in the outer walls to a cesspit. Neither piety nor hygiene demanded such amenities in the average sixteenth-century farmhouse, let alone the fourteenth-century.

One clue to age in timber-framed buildings is the space between the studs, although this could be affected by the availability of timber and the local demand for it. Generally speaking, the closer the timbers the older the house. When timber became scarce and costly, the spaces between the studs were widened to form panels rather than strips and were infilled with wattle and daub. Later, however, close-studding was reintroduced for the ostentatious display of wealth, especially along the Welsh Marches.

The much-photographed farmhouse overlooking the village pond and stocks at Albury in Hertfordshire is a perfect example of the evolution of the smaller English farmhouse at the end of the sixteenth-century. In the middle is the close-timbered Elizabethan farmhouse, with a crudely constructed extension in which timber is sparingly used. At the other end is a seventeenth-century wing with a fine chamber on the upper floor and massive external chimney-stack. In this wing timber is used only to conform in style with the rest of the building.

The decisive revolution in building styles came with the introduction of chimneys. William Harrison in his *Description of England* (1577) says: 'There are old men yet dwelling in the village where I remain which have noted three things to be marvellously altered in England within their sound remembrance ... One is the multitude of chimneys lately erected'. This innovation meant that fireplaces could now be against either an inner or an outer wall, and as the smoke no longer drifted through the hall to accumulate into a cloud blackening the rafters, a floor could be inserted in the hall itself. So instead of the ladder or rough stairs built of logs cut from the trunks of trees hitherto used to reach upper floors, finely moulded staircases could be introduced as the main feature of the hall.

The other two alterations that Harrison's Radwinter parishioners had noticed in Essex were the improvement in living conditions and household furnishings. For these to be introduced, windows had to be glazed. The Anglo-Saxon word for window is *eag-thyrl*, 'eyehole'; the Old Norse is *vindauga*, 'wind-eye'. The one indicates the smallness of the first windows, the other the way the wind blew

20

through them – and also the basic difference between the practical terminology of the Saxon and the imaginative of the Norse. Diamond-shaped leaded windows, which have remained in favour for country cottages, were simply a refinement of the earlier wooden lattices made of withies woven diagonally. They were in this form because the diamond pattern had been found more effective than the square in keeping out the rain, which ran off the slanted sticks more quickly than off the horizontal. In fact, unglazed windows continued to be common in the poorer parts of England long after the introduction of glass, and did not go out of use in Wales until the end of the seventeenth century.

Before glass came into use, protection from severe weather was obtained with shutters, which were more effective than might be supposed. While farmhouses continued to be one room deep, shutters had only to be closed on the side from which the wind was blowing. Further protection came from the use of the kind of half-doors now chiefly associated with stables. These were called heck doors, a word that has the same meaning as hatch, or gate, and is still in use in the north of England for hay-racks and frames used for drying cheeses.

The introduction of these refinements would bring with it an awareness of discomforts, especially draughts, which must have increased when dairies and kitchens were built onto the back of the main living-room, with outer doors constantly opening and shutting. Screens – variously called speers, spurs, hecks and, in the Lake District, mells – were erected at the side of the fireplace to baffle the draught.

The earliest and still the most effective door-fastener was a bar that slid into a slot in either the outer wall or a jamb of the doorway. In the North of England this was called a stang – another word imported from Norway. These heavy sliding bars were superseded by shorter bars called snecks – yet another Scandinavian word – which were fixed with one end sufficiently loose to allow the other end to move up and down freely. At night the doors were secured by slipping into the staple above the sneck a peg called a snib, which when not in use hung at the side of the door on a piece of string or a leather thong.

If the question is asked: 'What can possibly be the interest in listing all these minor details of domestic architecture and trivial contrivances of three hundred years ago?', the answer is clear. In no other period of less than a single short lifetime have houses been built and furnished in styles that have so enduringly captivated the imagination of rich and poor in succeeding generations. The chairmakers of High Wycombe continue to exploit this nostalgia. So did the architect, C.F.A. Voysey, who in the present century made doors with snibs and snecks for indoor rooms, and front doors with boards butted against each other and held taut by long iron hinges. In the bedrooms he placed the windows directly below the eaves in lofty Edwardian rooms, both to minimize the draught and to admit maximum light, a device that had been used before windows were glazed. Hearths that were buried behind eighteenth- and nineteenth-century mantelpieces were opened up, and their brickwork was exposed and furnished with Sussex iron fireplates, firedogs and alcoves to store logs in. Cumbrian court cupboards, Welsh dressers, gate-legged tables, ladder-backed chairs and linen chests from seventeenth-century farm kitchens, as well as every conceivable utensil in brass and pewter, continue to fetch prices in auction sales that would have astounded our grandparents.

On the other hand, we can no longer face up to the kind of meals described by such writers as Gervase Markham, to whom a 'humble feast' might include 'sixteen dishes of meat that are of substance and not emptie, or for shew'. For great occasions would be added 'sallets, fricases, quelque-choses, and devised paste, as many dishes more, which make the full service no lesse than two-and-thirtie dishes'.

This sudden accession of wealth, such as had never before been dreamed of, came to England in the wake of economic liberation from generations of stagnation under the rule of the abbots. Prices rose so rapidly after the last of the abbeys was dissolved in 1540 that by 1570 the social revolution was in full spate, with all the changes in country living that Harrison describes so vividly.

The reigns of Elizabeth I and James I witnessed the building of England's finest minor domestic architecture. But in the chimney corners of these enlarged farmhouses, with walls hung with tapestries, cupboards stocked with plate, tables set with pewter on fine napery, and all apparently going merrily as a marriage bell, the old men wagged their heads as old men will and prophesied a sombre day of reckoning. And it came, as it always does. With the outbreak of the Civil War, to use our twentieth-century expression, 'the party was over'.

The tide would have ebbed even if the Civil War had not broken out. While wealth had been accumulating in the hands of those who gained possession of the monastic estates and their local agents, the labourer's lot had not improved. A few hovels built of granite or rough moor stone have survived in the West and North-West of England to show how the poor lived. Elsewhere no cottages built for labourers in the fifteenth and sixteenth centuries exist today. What are sometimes sold as such are farmhouses that had been split up in the eighteenth-century in the manner already described. In very few parts of England are there genuine labourers' cottages of periods earlier than the eighteenth century. But we have descriptions of earlier ones. One of the best is by Bishop Hall (1574-1656), who described the labourer's cottage as being still

> Of one bay's breadth, God wot, a silly cote
> Whose thatched spars are furred with sluttish soote
> A whole inch thick, shining like blackmoor's brows,
> Through smoke that downe the headlesse barrel blows.
> At his bed's feete feeden his stalled teame,
> The swine beneath, his pullen o'er the beame.
>
> Joseph Hall, *Satires* (1598)

But wretched as these hovels were, and envious as those who lived in them became of the wealth of the men who employed them, few labourers starved except in the severest winter weather. The population was small and the copses teemed with life. There were plenty of rabbits and birds to be snared for the pot, every cottage would have a bit of cultivated ground to grow vegetables in, and many had a pig in a sty at the rear. While the farmer's wife grew sweet williams, lupins, scabious and hollyhocks, the labourer's wife would search the hedgerows for plants to provide the household remedies that make old herbals such stimulating reading, with their recommendations of such nostrums as brews from fennel for weak eyes, camomile for headaches, lilies to break the bile, goats-rue brewed in ale to ward off the plague, and aniseed

23

for 'opening the pipes'. In addition to baking and brewing, smoking ham and bottling wine by day, the women had spinning and embroidery to keep them busy in the long evenings.

While the building of fine houses ceased during the Civil War in the South, a large number of stone farmhouses were built from about 1650 in the Midlands stone belt and as far north as the Lake District. In the Home Counties the farmers suffered less than the gentry during the struggle between King and Parliament. There were more farmers on Cromwell's side than on the King's. With the gentry, who were fewer of course, the proportions would be reversed. If we look up inventories of well-to-do-yeomen who died late in the seventeenth-century, we see how greatly their possessions had increased during the Commonwealth. It may be that many of the gentry who had supported the King had been obliged to sell their goods to clear debts, and these had been bought by their own tenant farmers.

The final great period of farmhouse building came with the Enclosure Acts of the eighteenth century. Much of the land in the peripheral English counties – those along the south and east coasts and the Welsh Marches – had been enclosed earlier, with Essex, Kent and Devon, in what the old antiquaries referred to as 'time out of mind'. Planned enclosures had started in the fourteenth-century, with lords of manors fencing in the demesne lands in the middle of which they lived in their manor houses. Setting aside all the arguments about the moral rights or wrongs of what happened at the time, it is now accepted that the imposed control of labour under the manorial system paved the way for the leadership by which progressive landowners in all parts of England brought their tenant farmers out of non-progressive agriculture into the system that eventually enabled them to feed the nation during the Napoleonic Wars.

This new-found prosperity led to the third and last great period of farmhouse rebuilding. Seventeenth-century farmhouses in most parts of England had continued to be one room deep, with extensions at one or both ends and outshuts at the rear. In the late eighteenth and early nineteenth centuries they were doubled in depth. This was most easily achieved, if the landowner could afford the expense, by building an entirely new house in which chimneys, rooms, hall and staircase could be planned in logical proportions of brick in the south of England, stone in the north and south-west. Many built at this time are still called Brickhouse or Stonehouse Farm. Considered as a plan, the Georgian farmhouse, simple as it is, has never been bettered from the point of view of convenience, particularly when such working quarters as dairies and brewhouses were relegated to ancillary buildings.

A large proportion of these new farmhouses were built to adaptations of plans in pattern-books imported from the Continent. They can be found in every part of England, each providing its own commentary on local farming prosperity and landowning involvement, particularly as battles seem to have been curiously popular events for celebrating in this way: Blenheim, Bunker's Hill, Inkerman, Trafalgar, and Waterloo came to mind as examples. Pattern-books for farmhouses appear to have begun to circulate widely about the middle of the eighteenth century. The first to be produced by a British architect was one by Daniel Garrett, published in 1747.

These new farmhouses became increasingly commodious as time went on, and eminent architects entered the field with elaborate plans for entire farmsteads, with buildings ranged round foldyards at the rear, along with orchards and kitchen gardens enclosed by high brick walls in the best manor-house style. Enterprising publishers co-operated with what we now call blurbs, addressing farmers in flattering terms as 'Noblemen and Gentlemen'. New words, such as 'farmery' were introduced, and to take the farmer's mind off the grim associations of winter nights in 'byres', 'shippons' and 'mistals', cowhouses were called 'cow-parlours'!

The man who jumped on the bandwagon most effectively was John Claudius Loudon (1783-1843), the son of a Lanarkshire farmer who must have had prophetic powers in choosing for his son so imperial a name. Loudon was as prolific a writer on all things rural in the nineteenth century as Gervase Markham had been in the seventeenth, and he expanded the range of professional know-how by editing magazines and compiling encyclopaedias at breath-taking speed. His *Encyclopaedia of Cottage, Farm and Villa Architecture* was a compendium of twelve hundred pages to which more than fifty experts contributed. There was to be no limit to farmhouse aggrandizement. Even the smallest should have one parlour, and farms of more than three hundred acres should have two, in addition to a 'library', in which farmhouse business should be conducted, just as every squire JP had a 'Justice Room' in his house. At one stage in his career Loudon edited five journals simultaneously. Today his memorial is to be seen in Oxfordshire, where the beautiful village of Great Tew was built as part of his replanning of the local farming system while agent for the owner of the land.

In this new world of affluence, with incomes suddenly expanded to support an inflated way of life, farmers came into line with the clergy, who, with the increased income they were deriving from tithes, were able to build themselves rectories as elegant as the manor-house style farmhouses built by their churchwardens. So while the elderly looked back nostalgically to the dimly lit, low-beamed farmhouses of their youth, with blazing logs on open hearths, the young were able to disport themselves in Jane Austen type withdrawing-rooms, with the light pouring in through sash or bow windows to show off their Chippendale or Sheraton furniture, their silver cups and Worcester china.

1. *Cob and Thatch*

Cob and thatch, Harpford, Newton Poppleford

As the most primitive form of walling, cob must always have been 'the poor man's masonry', and Bede's reference (in the year 642) to thatch roofing should surprise no one, since if we are overtaken by heavy rain while walking in the country we creep under a hedge for shelter. The marvel is that thatch should have continued for so long in favour in the affluent South of England. In most parts of the North it was superseded by stone slab or slate more than two hundred years ago.

The primitive form of thatch would be the mixture of rough grass, bracken and ling that still sheltered shepherds on the

27

Lakeland fells when Wordsworth walked them. Since then the material used for thatching farmhouses and cottages is less easily identifiable from records because – whereas in East Anglia, for example, 'reeds' are the stems of the vigorous aquatic plants that grow on Norfolk marshes – in the West of England reeds are unthreshed wheat, which in Devon continues to be used for coping farmyard walls as well as for roofing farmhouses.

Wheat for thatching, fortunately, has always been treated with great care. It continued to be cut with a sickle to avoid damaging the fibres long after cutting-machines had come into use, and it is still cut in that way by conscientious landowners. On National Trust estates straw is grown specially for thatching where there is no risk of its being weakened by fertilizers.

The first agricultural writer to give instructions on thatching was Henry Best, who farmed at Elmswell in East Yorkshire. I have always remembered his advice that 'wette straw' is easier on the thatcher's hands and 'coucheth better and beddes closer' since being drawn into a discussion on the probable origin of a small pit in the Cotswolds which turned out to have been a pond used for soaking straw in preparation for thatching. In addition to the reasons for soaking given by Henry Best, the old thatchers used to soak their straw in a solution of water and alum to reduce the risk of fire. In East Anglia, the Norfolk Broads provided the water for soaking. After being cut with scythes, Norfolk reeds are floated downstream from the Broads to a convenient place for stacking until the folded leaves fall off them. They are then left to 'season' before being ready for the thatcher, who practises a craft that has normally been handed down from father to son through many generations.

To ensure that rainwater ran off the thatch as quickly as possible, there was a tradition in some parts of Devon for roofs to be pitched at an angle of not less than sixty degrees, and nowhere at less than fifty. In Norfolk, where rainfall is low, they might be pitched at forty degrees. In eastern England the enemy is the wind that blows in from the North Sea. So while in the West of England thatched roofs were pleasantly rounded at the corners (wrapped, one might say, round the shoulders), in East Anglia the ends of the walls were built up in stiff-backed gables, with the thatch tightly bedded between them to keep out the wind.

The thatcher starts work at the eaves and finishes with a broad band securely pinned along the ridge, usually with a scalloped edge. The bundles are laid in wide bands across laths and rafters and stitched together with steel needles threaded with tarred twine. Formerly they were pegged down with hazel sticks approximately two feet long, sharpened at the ends and twisted to hairpin shape so that they could be driven into the thatch like staples. In East Anglia they were called sprinkles or sprindles, in other places spelks. It used to be said that the bundles, when finished, were so closely packed that the roof looked like the fur on an animal's back.

As reeds were collected in mid-winter, when the Broads were fully exposed to biting winds cutting across them, reeding (from which the common East Anglian surname Reeder is derived) was not the most enviable of occupations. So it is hardly surprising that rye grass has been widely cultivated for thatching even in Norfolk, which is still the county in which it can be seen at its best, although Suffolk now claims to have more thatched roofs than any other county in England, and the proportion is still high in north Essex and Cambridgeshire.

Thatched roofs are now expensive luxuries when they have to be insured against fire. When I expressed regret recently to an architect friend on seeing the thatch being removed from a romantic 'Willy Lot' style cottage in north Essex, and preparations being made for tiling, he told me that the sole reason for this was what he described as 'the prohibitive cost of insuring thatch'. This is a very different state of affairs from that described in an article in *The Architects' Journal* of 12 December, 1923, which referred to the thatch on a smithy near Cambridge on which sparks had fallen daily for seventy years without damage, and to a fire in a thatched house not only failing to ignite the thatch but actually being extinguished when the roof collapsed on the blazing interior. For all that, thatched roofs did catch fire, and many village greens along the east coast originated not in Saxon commons but in clearings left after huddled cottages had been destroyed by fires whipped to fury by the spring gales. The nine greens at Southwold in Suffolk were cleared in this way, and 'fire hooks' for pulling the thatch off blazing roofs to prevent the fire spreading are kept in many village

churches. There is also one in St Benet's at Cambridge. In fact, fires
in thatched roofs usually arise, even now, not externally but from
defects in the brickwork of the chimney-stack, allowing soot to
collect on ledges.

In the seventeenth century it was acknowledged that wind did
more damage than fire. Celia Fiennes, who visited Cornwall
towards the end of the century, describes the gales that blew in
from angry seas at Redruth: 'I perceive they are very bleake in these
countryes especially to this north ocean and the winds so
troublesome they are forced to spin straw and so make a caul or net
worke to lay over their thatch on the ricks and outhouses, with
waites of stones round to defend the thatch from being blown away
by the greate winds; not but they have a better way of thatching
their houses with reeds and so close that when its well done will
last twenty years, but what I mention of braces or bands of straw is
on their rickes which is only to hold a yeare.' The problem
continues and extends to farmhouses as well as ricks. In the Fens
old fishnets used to be thrown over the roof and pegged into the
thatch. Now wire netting is used, but mainly as protection against
birds trying to burrow-nest or pull out ears of corn, as corn
buntings will if given the chance.

Although West Country thatching is inferior to the reed
thatching of Norfolk, cob and thatch are still seen at their best in
combination in Devon, Somerset and Dorset, where long-settled
families like the Welds of Dorset and the Aclands of Devon have
been meticulously conscientious in maintaining them. The cob
farmhouses of these counties, of which the most typical are
seventeenth-century, were all built by the same basic method, with
local variations in ways of 'packing' the cob.

The well-known West Country saying that all that cob needs for
long life is a good hat and a good pair of shoes takes account of the
heavy rainfall of the South-West. The 'hat' is the thatch that must
come far enough over the eaves to allow the rainwater to clear the
walls. The 'shoes' in Devon and Cornwall are a plinth of blocks of
moor stone built, ideally, to a height of $2\frac{1}{2}$ feet, then packed with
cob. From this stone foundation, which is regularly tarred to keep it
effective as a damp course, the walls are built up in layers of two
feet thick and approximately $2\frac{1}{2}$ feet high between shutters fixed

together to form troughs into which the cob was shovelled after being trodden out by oxen to firm consistency.

The formula for mixing cob in Cornwall was one part broken slate to two parts clay, with barley straw to bind them. In both Devon and Cornwall the traditional proportions were eight bundles of barley straw — one packhorse load — trodden into nine cartloads of clay. Each layer was left for a week or more, according to the weather, to dry out before another layer was added, so building was a slow process. Doors and window-frames were fitted in as the walls went up, the mason and his men pounding the cob against each frame to make the fitting firm and water-tight. The weakest points were always the corners. In woodland districts these were given timber supports; in the South-West, where straight timber was scarce, they were usually rounded to reduce the danger of abrasion or crumbling. In Cornwall it was said that the corners were shaved off so that there would be no nooks for the Devil to hide in.

Cob was always less suitable for the exposed villages of Cornwall than for the combes of Devon, where whole villages are built entirely of it and are still as trim and fresh in appearance as when they were built three or four hundred years ago. They are in such perfect harmony with their close-fitting environment that the countryside would be despoiled if they were replaced by modern buildings, even of local stone. Newton St Cyres on the Crediton road out of Exeter, Atherton and Broad Hembury spring to mind as among the best of the many villages either entirely or almost entirely built of cob. They bask throughout the summer months secure and neighbourly under the low thatched roofs that cast such beautiful shadows as the sun sinks behind them.

Despite the slowness of building in cob, the traditional method continued to be followed into the nineteenth century. But Vancouver, in his 1808 *Survey of Devon* for the Board of Agriculture, reported that recently a new wash had come into use for preserving the rough cast and had become customary as a final coating for the cob. He gave the recipe for this as 'four parts of pounded lime, three of sand, two of pounded wood ashes, and one of scoria of iron, mixed well together and made sufficiently fluid to be applied with a brush'. He assured the Board that 'When dry it gives the appearance of new Portland stone, and affords an excellent protection against the penetrating force of the south-westerly storms.' Cob building continues in the West of England. Its merits were examined enthusiastically by Clough Williams-Ellis and by John and Elizabeth Eastwick-Field, in a book entitled *Building in Cob, Pise and Stabilised Earth (Country Life,* 1947). Just before the 1914-18 War an exceptionally fine cob house was built by Ernest Gimson near Budleigh Salterton, using stiff sand found on the site bound together with water and great quantities of wheat straw on a plinth of cobble stones sifted out of the sand.

The extraordinarily high standard maintained for cob farmhouses in the South-West may have been influenced by the local custom of granting life-leases, which in practice meant security of tenure not only for the tenant to whom the lease was granted but for his family for generations. In effect it was comparable with the 'customary tenancies' of Cumbria. The weakness in the system was that sooner or later black sheep turn up in all families, and if such a tenancy fell into irresponsible hands, the weakness in the cob as well as the law was exposed. Neglected foundations became honeycombed with rat holes, walls bulged and thatches let in the rain.

Probably the best-known cob farmhouse in the South-West of England is Hayes Barton, a mile out of East Budleigh, the birthplace of Sir Walter Raleigh, who wrote of it: 'For ye naturall disposition I have to that place being born in that house, I had rather see myself there than anywhere else.' Eden Phillpotts reported that in his day, although 'patched and tinkered through the centuries ... it still endures, complete and sturdy, in harmony of old design, with unspoilt dignity from a far past'.

Devon has been especially favoured in having writers with a feeling for local style. The best was Sabine Baring-Gould, squarson of Lewtrenchard, a village smothered in a Devon combe, to whom the earth was 'a book of the history of mankind'. He loved nothing better than to call on one of his elderly parishioners and share a meal of newly baked scones, pastry and cups of tea over a gossip about village life when both were young. He was not a hunting parson, though his children rode and the Lamerton hounds would sometimes meet at Lew House, with hounds and horses assembled round the flowing fountain, huntsmen and riders in pink coats being served with sandwiches and cherry brandy. No one knew better than Baring-Gould how much Devon folk treasured their cob houses, cool in summer and warm in winter. In his *Book of the West* he wrote: 'I have known labourers bitterly bewail their fate in being transferred from an old fifteenth- or sixteenth-century cob cottage into a newly built stone edifice of the most approved style, as they said it was like going out of warm life into a cold grave.' Of cob garden walls he wrote: 'Cob walls for garden fruit are incomparable. They retain the warmth of the sun and give it out through the night ... when protected by slates, tiles, or thatch [they] will last for centuries.'

Cob farmhouses as well as cottages are found along the entire length of the ancient routes across the Downs out of Dorset, where the clay and chalk were bound together with straw on ploughed land and heather on heath. Sand and gravel were used more in Dorset than in Devon for strengthening, but everywhere the most effective bonding material was horsehair when trodden into clay.

In Wiltshire the base material of cob was chalk, which had the initial advantage of being drier and stronger than clay. Some of the strongest surviving cob walls are found on analysis to consist of three parts ground-up chalk to one part clay, with straw kneaded or trodden into it. At Winterslow, north-east of Salisbury, where the best chalk-mud buildings in Wiltshire may be seen, the chalk is close to the surface, so could be dug out with a spade when required for building. The pit made in the process would then fill with water and serve as a well. Many of these pits were later lined with concrete to ensure that the water supply remained free from seepage.

In the final stages of erection the walls in both Devon and Wiltshire houses looked much the same and had to be scraped down to a smooth surface with a flat iron shovel called a paring iron. The side used against the wall was flat throughout the length of both handle and blade, so resembled the peels, or shovels, used by old-time bakers to draw batches of loaves out of ovens. Before they were lime-washed, it was essential that such chalk-mud walls as those in Wiltshire should be given a good skin of plaster, since chalk absorbs water freely and crumbles quickly.

Chalk-mud farmhouses of the same consistency are found all along the Downs as they run out of Wiltshire through Hampshire, particularly in the villages round Andover. In the Amesbury district of Wiltshire chalk-mud walling has continued in favour but brick quoins have been introduced for house walls, especially round windows and doors, and to strengthen external angles. Brick chimney-stacks are now universal in the Downs, and where hipped roofs were not practicable because of the exposed nature of the site, the tip of the gables might still be hipped to form a gablet.

Travelling eastward across the chalk belt, the impression strengthens that chalk in general is too soft to be built with and is best used as a thickening agent. Clunch, however, the hard chalk from the lower deposits associated chiefly with the countryside north of the Thames, had the advantage of being capable of being cut into blocks and used like brick. This is the material that when given a durable skin of plaster and several coats of colour-wash has all the appearance of West Country cob and is found along both sides of the Icknield Way out of Buckinghamshire into East Anglia.

East of this we get the ancient form of cob called clay-lump, which was, in fact, used in prehistoric times in Egypt and Mesopotamia. It was produced in the usual way by treading straw into clay from which the larger stones had been removed, but when the required consistency had been obtained, the mixture was shovelled into wooden frames, or moulds, measuring eighteen inches long by nine inches wide and six inches deep, for use in external walls. The frames were then laid out in the sun for the clay to dry, which means that clay-lumps were in effect sun-dried bricks. When ready, they were built up in walls only half the thickness of the cob walls of Devon, and on completion were plastered and washed with brilliant colours, of which terra-cotta has always been the most popular. The strong traditional colour was obtained by mixing the red juice of sloes with the black juice of damsons.

The reason why this method of building is practically confined to East Anglia in England is that the rainfall there is lowest and the drying winds are strongest. These in combination made it possible to build clay-lump walls up to roof height in days, or at most weeks, when in Devon it might take weeks if not months for each layer of cob to dry out. East Anglia does, of course, have some rain, and when blown in from the sea it can penetrate the thickest wall, so as a final precaution clay-lump walls were often tarred, and when the tar was nearly dry, sand was thrown on them, which in turn might be concealed by colour-wash.

The best places to see cottages and farmhouses built of clay-lump are the villages on boulder clay south of Wymondham and between Thetford and Diss in Norfolk, and the villages on boulder clay in Cambridgeshire. They are unique in England, and whether under thatch or Dutch pantiles have great attraction in their sharp angles and bright planes; but no doubt most people would feel that they lack the charm of the rounded corners, softly curving lines along the eaves when under thatch, and the tall, hipped roofs of Dorset and Devon.

The other traditional form of farmhouse building in eastern England is in wattle and daub. The wattle panels are formed of interwoven hazel sticks and were sprung into position between the studs of timber-framed buildings by having holes drilled into the timber frame to take the pointed ends of the staves sideways, and grooves to take them lengthways. The plastering, or daubing, of these panels developed into a highly sophisticated local art during the seventeenth-century. More straw was used for wattle and daub construction than for cob, and dung was added to prevent the clay cracking. As with cob, daub panels have proved remarkably durable if patched regularly to keep out the rain.

The use of cleft oak laths as an alternative to split hazel sticks developed into lath-and-plaster walling, which became a distinctive local feature in the chalk districts of west Suffolk, north Essex and east Hertfordshire. In contrast to the thick cob walls of Dorset and Devon, these lath-and-plaster walls of East Anglia are surprisingly thin. Six inches is common in farmhouse walls, as little as four inches in cottage and interior walls. The most typical of these lath-and-plaster panels are in the wings of timber-framed hall-houses, which if the hall timbers are secured by wooden pegs and have genuine adze marks along the main beams, means that the core of the house is probably Tudor. If the wings are early and original, they will probably be wattle and daub, the wattle being hazel sticks with the bark still on them, packed with clay and coated

A pargeted house, Clare, Suffolk

with lime plaster. The lath-and-plaster of the larger seventeenth-century farmhouses have flatter surfaces, which local builders soon discovered gave them greater scope for ornamentation. When strengthened with both horsehair and cowdung, the plaster was found to be strong enough to be moulded into symmetrical panels, which could be decorated with patterns by craftsmen called pargeters, who evolved a form of vernacular art which reached a high degree of skill in parts of Suffolk and north Essex.

Pargeting evolved in three stages. The earliest patterns were either pricked or scratched in the plaster with a comb in shapes of which arrowheads, tortoiseshells, zigzags, scallops and basketwork were the favourites. Sometimes small moulds like those on butter-pats were used. In these, interlaced squares were common. Then came the Jacobean strapwork patterns squeezed onto the plaster by the method now used by confectioners for icing cakes, and finally the elaborate symbolic designs seen in such ancient towns as Saffron Walden in Essex and Lavenham and Ipswich in Suffolk, where the favourite motif was the mitre of Bishop Blaize, the patron saint of woolcombers.

The best pargeting was done after the Restoration of Charles II in 1660, but such early designs as the pomegranate, the emblem of Catherine of Aragon (on a ceiling in Monks Soham in Suffolk), the Tudor rose on old inns, and the *fleur-de-lis* or bishop's mitre on former guildhalls, all indicate a high degree of skill in the sixteenth century. They were probably the work of Italian plasterers commissioned to decorate guildhalls. Where such work appears on inns and farmhouses – some of which were formerly inns – we may suspect that it was done to settle scores with the innkeeper.

2. Farm Life in the South-West

Beehive oven, Warwick

Volcanic action has played odd tricks with England's rock formation. The granite and slate found in the extreme South-West turn up again in the fells of Cumbria, giving these widely separated regions common features in their vernacular architecture – notably in the massive crow-stepped chimneystacks built against the outer walls of the old farmhouses, capped with the cylindrical chimneys that Wordsworth claimed for Westmorland with such proprietory fervour.

The explanation of most of the architectural features found in both is that the granite quarried in Cornwall and Cumbria, especially in Shap, is too hard to be worked for clean-cut architecture, and the slate rubble, when well bedded in lime mortar, becomes almost as hard as granite. The charm of both regions is that the rock is so near the surface that landscape and buildings are in strikingly intimate relationship. The differences between them, which are no less striking on close scrutiny, are historical. They spring from Norse influence in Cumbria, Continental in Cornwall.

As Continental influence has been the stronger over England as a whole, Cornwall should be looked at first. Chysauster, near Penzance, has the remains of an Iron Age street of farmhouses, each one built of granite with two oval-shaped rooms, one for family, the other for livestock. These remarkable survivals, built two thousand years ago, represent in embryo both the longhouse, with family and cattle under one continuous roof, and the quadrangular farmstead which the Romans imported from Gaul. Although the latter was to become chiefly associated with lowland regions, it must have been established early in the Devon 'bartons'.

Continental influences were indicated four hundred years ago by Richard Carew, who in his *Survey of Cornwall* (1602) wrote: 'The ancient Cornish manner of building was to plant their houses low, making their walls thick, their windows arched and little, seeking only strength and warmness; whereas nowadays they seat their dwellings high, build their walls thin, and mould their lights large, seeking chiefly prospect and pleasure'. Nothing like that could have been written about Cumbria until more than a hundred years later. To have achieved such a change of attitude in the South-West by the end of the sixteenth-century was evidence that the squires and gentry of Cornwall – all practical farmers with valuable minerals under the surface of their land – had adopted a degree of sophistication in their manner of life that could have come only from Europe.

Within Cornwall itself two distinct building traditions evolved. The old farmhouses of the south already were, and continued to be, built of granite when not of cob. Usually they had a plantation of beech trees near them to act as a wind-break, in the way Cumbrian farms had a plantation of sycamores in post-medieval times. They were the farmhouses that figure in Cornish romances down to those of Sir Arthur Quiller-Couch and Daphne du Maurier in the twentieth century. Those in the north were most likely to be built of slate, and slate of such quality that at Delabole, three miles south-west of Camelford, the effect is startling. The entire village is of slate, and the surrounding fields are framed with walls in which thick slates are laid in herringbone fashion with as much ingenuity as the masons of the Cotswolds laid their slabs, and as much birough as North Country masons used to build their drystone walls. Each region, of course, had its special problems. Cornwall's was the ferocity of Atlantic gales, which meant that every crevice in the walls had to be packed with earth or mortar to secure them from the worst that storm could do to them. The associated problem was to ensure that rainwater drained away as quickly as possible. For this purpose the slope of herringbone construction in walling was found more effective than horizontal coursing.

House roofs were a related problem, solved by two different devices. One was the standard method of laying the heaviest slates along the eaves to support the progressively thinner ones in the courses above them. The other was to set the slates edge to edge, sealing the joints with bitumen or tar. Today many are laid in cement and washed over with a cement slurry, which unfortunately excludes air as well as rain. Again as in the Lake District, slate is used in Cornwall for wall-cladding. Like the weatherboarding of the south-east of England this became fashionable as well as protective in the eighteenth century.

All these features contribute to Cornwall's grey, austere landscape, sculptured and moulded by Nature and modified by man in his external contest with the weather for survival. As for livestock, what Herdwick sheep are to the fells of Cumbria, stags to the Highlands, and black cattle to Wales, goats – at least traditionally – are to Cornwall.

But Cornwall is not all rough grazing and Atlantic gales. Its farm life has rich domestic traditions. Today we associate scalded cream with Devon rather than Cornwall, but Cornishmen claim that the art of making it was learned by their own ancestors from the Phoenicians who traded with the Cornish for tin, and that Devon folk stole the secret formula for making it from them. The claim may be thought to find support in that cream is obtained by the old Cornish method in Iran today, although the truth is that what is claimed to be the original method of making Cornish cream in the dairies of the fertile valleys of the south is extremely rare anywhere now. However, the tradition still lingers in Cornwall that it was originally made by a process in which the milk, after being strained, was left to stand in shallow pans for between twelve and twenty-four hours, to give the cream time to rise to the top before being heated slowly over a peat fire until the cream began to show a raised ring round the edges. The pans were then carried back to the dairy and left for another twelve hours to allow the yellow crust to settle, the greatest care being taken not to break it.

Later, charcoal stoves were used, and later again the milk was poured into tin pans inserted into an outer pan filled with boiling water to scald the cream. William Marshall was of the opinion that this was the local method for collecting cream for butter-making before churns were introduced, when clots of cream were beaten by hand until the butter came.* In both Devon and Cornwall 'separators' are now used to isolate the cream for scalding.

The association with Cornwall exclusively of the pasty, which provides a balanced meal to satisfy the healthiest appetite, is often disputed. It is said to be explained by Cornish miners' carrying a taste for the meal to the Rand when so many emigrated to work in the goldfields. The true Cornish pasty was different from others in that all the ingredients – beef steak, calf's liver, potatoes, onions and the rest – were assembled raw and baked and cooked together.

With Cornish fisherman fish pies were naturally more popular than meat pasties, especially when heavily seasoned with salt and pepper to stimulate a healthy thirst. Charles Kingsley in *Hereward the Wake* described squab pie, which he says was made up of layers of apple, bacon, onions and mutton, with 'a squab or young cormorant which diffused through the pie and through the ambient air a delicate odour of mingled guano and polecat'. The alternative of young cormorant is resented by Cornishmen, and scorned as evidence of ignorance, since in Cornwall everybody knows 'squab' exclusively means young pigeon.

The average Englishman, sitting down to a meal in a Cornish farmhouse thirty or forty years ago, was shocked to see his host pouring cream on a savoury pie. Apparently this is an old Cornish custom. A work entitled *Art of Cookery* compiled in Cornwall has the lines:

Our fathers most admired their sauces sweet
And often asked for sugar with their meat,

Rural Economy of England, 1798

41

They buttered currants on fat veal bestowed
And rumps of beef with virgin honey strowed.
Hence mackerel seem delightful to the eyes,
Tho' dressed with incoherent gooseberries.

Fish figures in most Cornish dishes, just as bacon does in many parts of England and cheese in Wales. Pilchards, hake, cod and skate were always available, since they were dried and smoked in the deep open fireplaces of Cornish kitchens, then laid on racks between the ceiling beams.

Cornish kitchens had much in common with Welsh in their furnishing. The dresser was the housewife's pride in both, but in Cornwall the greatest pride was in its display of pewter plates and mugs made from local tin. Another interesting link with Wales is in the use in both of the word 'laity' for dairy or milkhouse.

When we cross the Tamar into Devon, we have Professor W.G. Hoskins to guide us, and no one who knows Devon in depth will dispute his claim that Dartmoor 'contains one of the most instructive collections of ancient farmhouses south of the Scottish Highlands, possibly in the whole of Great Britain'; but not all the most ancient are still occupied. The prosperous farmers of Devon did as much rebuilding as most in the late sixteenth and early seventeenth centuries, but as there was abundant moor stone available for new houses, the old ones were often left to serve as farm buildings, and sometimes the foundations of still older farmhouses can be discovered below the rubble dumped in a nearby field.

Professor Hoskins singles out Cholwith Town, in the parish of Cornwood, as a good specimen of a Tudor yeoman's house, with the remains of an older building in the yard. The difficulty in ascribing ownership may arise when one tries to date these ruins, although in this case documentary evidence exists which makes it virtually certain that the older building was the homestead of a member of the Cholwich family who owned the farm between 1200 and 1230. An old house at Stiniel in the parish of Chagford appears first in a document of *c.*1224.

The first farmhouses in Devon to start a continuous style seem to have been the long, narrow buildings found along the gentler hill slopes, usually with a southerly aspect, which are the West of

England type of longhouse. Like those in the North, they were built with the farmhouse at the upper end, the cattle byre at the lower, so that the slurry could drain away downhill and not pass along the front of the dwelling. A curious feature of lowland farmhouses in Devon is that the front door is often so low that it is necessary to stoop on entering, and then to descend one or two steps before reaching the through passage, which has the parlour – where Devon cream teas are served in summer – on one side and the kitchen either on the other or in an outshut at the rear. No doubt there is an explanation of doors being so low, but it is a feature that always seems odd when found in villages through which water flows swiftly down deep gutters from moorland immediately behind the village, particularly where it is freely admitted that flooding is endemic.

Many of these village farmhouses in south Devon are of red cob and were originally single-storeyed, with steeply pitched thatched roofs. When chimneys were built either into or onto them, they were placed against the long wall in order to heat both the living-room and the farmer's bedroom, which was built into the roof about the same time. When this was done in the seventeenth century, a dormer window was usually inserted in the thatch to light the best bedroom, with small windows in the gables for other bedrooms. Porches would probably come in about the same time, and by the middle of the seventeenth century they might even have an upper storey for use as a wool store.

The most typical element in farmhouse names in Devon is Barton, which in the sixteenth century usually indicated a demesne farm. Most of the bartons are still the best farms in their parishes and of manor-house status. Among the finest is Colleton Barton, near Chumleigh.

The West Country farmhouses most familiar to tourists are those in the Exmoor villages on the old Acland estates, now, through the generosity of the fifteenth baronet, Sir Richard, the property of the National Trust. They are usually built of cob or rubble. Many continue to be thatched and to have external chimney-stacks and deep-set latticed windows. In the larger villages the old farmhouses usually have a gable to the street, with a barn lengthways alongside them.

Bossington has always been a favourite of mine. It has one or two of the best farmhouses in Exmoor and beautifully kept simple cottages. Some of these have exceptionally wide doorways. I remember an elderly villager coming up to me while I was leaning on my stick trying to reconstruct its history. He explained that the doors were so wide because originally they opened into a corridor through which oxen brought in from the fields passed to reach the foldyard at the rear, and they had to take both the bulk of the beast and the spread of its great horns.

Although it is recognized that Devon oxen were famous for the exceptional size of their horns, there are other explanations of wide through passages. Professor M.W. Barley, in *The English Farmhouse*, while acknowledging that most of them were built in that way to take the oxen through, says that in at least one, Brook Farm, Clapton in Gordano, the doorways were 'widened about three feet above the ground, in order to get larger cider barrels into the house and through the hall'.

All the cottages in these villages originally had the half-circular protrusions roofed like beehives built into external chimney-stacks. Many retain them. They are baking-ovens, introduced into the West Country during the seventeenth century when fresh bread became a staple item in diet. In farmhouses another chamber was built in at a level lower than the fire grate, for smoking bacon. This would probably be introduced in the eighteenth century. It had a separate flue leading into the main chimney under a projecting roof. Yet another oven was built into the thick cob wall at a distance from the fireplace, for pans of cream to be placed in for scalding and clotting.

What is now regarded as Exmoor vernacular architecture was evolved by generations of the Acland family, who were landowners in Devon for eight hundred years and ruled over thousands of acres benevolently, if not always popularly, by following the dictates of conscience rather than fashion. Under the ninth baronet, who succeeded to the estates in 1785, Holnicote was always full of guests, with hunters in the stables for all who came. But he died at the age of thirty, to be succeeded by the tenth baronet (1787-1871) when only seven years old, and it was he who introduced into what was then a bleak landscape the vast plantations which have brought such mellow beauty to the foothills. It is estimated that between 1810 and 1826 he planted 800,000 trees around Holnicote and Winsford and established miles of footpaths across Exmoor, which were kept open by estate pensioners settled in the picturesque cottages round Selworthy Green, built to a design of his own but probably influenced by those in *Rural Architecture* (1823) by P.F. Robinson.

Sir Thomas, the eleventh baronet (1809-98), was the most enlightened of this remarkable line of landowners. As a brilliant scholar and accomplished artist, he might have been thought the wrong man to be an Exmoor landowner, particularly as he had no interest in the rough sporting life of the neighbouring squires and regarded deer as an unmitigated nuisance. In 1877 he became so incensed by their depredations on all the farming improvements he had introduced that he discussed getting rid of them entirely, but hesitated. After all, if the farmers were willing to put up with them, why should he complain? Money meant little to him. The local account of how he came to abandon the scheme is that on one occasion when he was discussing it, Lord Portsmouth, who was his guest at Killerton at the time, with superb diplomacy protested: 'No, no, don't do that. I find nothing so pacific as venison.' The effect of this was that a new pack was formed to replace the old one, and staghunting flourished on Exmoor as never before.

Sir Thomas was an ideal landlord, and most of the farmhouses on the fringe of the moor date from his reign. Tenancies were so eagerly sought, despite the severity of the climate, that only the keenest young farmers stood a chance of getting one. On being interviewed, an applicant might be asked how he would measure an oddly shaped field, what were the chemical constituents of dung, and similar questions for which he was entirely unprepared. Fortunately Sir Thomas did not expect him to know the answers. He was only interested to know whether the man before him was capable of acquiring the kind of knowledge that he thought would be a value. In short, he was really testing the mettle of the man. In fact, he described himself as 'one of those old-fashioned survivors of the pre-scientific period who was taught at Oxford by Aristotle that the only way to become a shoemaker was to make shoes'. Despite this he was the landowner who pioneered scientific agriculture in the West Country, largely by encouraging successful practical farmers to demonstrate their methods to their less enterprising neighbours.

His outstanding natural attribute was that he was able to maintain a balance between detachment and involvement, and advise those more economically affected than he was personally how 'to render science more practical and practice more scientific'. He never made personal advantage the deciding factor in the experiments conducted on his own farms, always recognizing that he, as a wealthy landowner, could afford to take risks in a way that his tenants, living hand to mouth by tilling the land and rearing stock in a harsh climate, could not. His reward was a long and healthy life and universal respect from his tenants, especially the farmers' wives. He knew that the most important work was done in the dairies, and those were the first places he poked his head into when visiting his farms. Knowing that this might be resented, he cultivated a knack of dropping useful hints while showing his ignorance of such matters as feeding a baby or doing a delicate piece of needlework, which gave the housewife an opportunity to score off him, and leave her with good stories of what she had been able to tell Sir Thomas the last time he called.

But the Aclands were not typical of the general run of hunting, shooting, fishing farmer-squires of Exmoor, who lived in square, commodious manor-houses like Cloutsham, Malmesmead and Bratton Court on the southern slope of North Hill, Minehead.

Moving eastward, between Minehead and Taunton, Exmoor merges into the flowing landscape of the Quantocks, where the lushness of the West Country envelops every farmstead. The farmhouses themselves are plain, but they are smothered in orchards that foam with blossom in spring and glow with fruit in autumn. The mind of the tourist turns from clotted cream to apples and cider, and to match this plenty the quarries yield stone for building as russet as the pippins in the orchards. The whole of the Quantocks country retains its rural integrity. Immediately east of the hills the stone is strong and enduring but dull, and throughout Somerset we find those sure indicators of monastic rather than lay influence: splendid tithe barns, among the best of which are those at Glastonbury, Wells, West Pennard and Preston Plunkett, near

Yeovil, all so different from the rudely constructed barns of Devon.

The masons and carpenters who built the noble church towers of Somerset – unsurpassed in England – were available after the Dissolution to build secular buildings. Somerset developed unevenly, but became a rich and fruitful county, and Bristol, itself a county as well as a city, disputed with Norwich the right to be accounted the second city in the kingdom. Farmers prospered along with merchants and in the second half of the seventeenth century built farmhouses as good as were built in most parts in the eighteenth.

Such enterprises as the draining of the peat fens of the Somerset Levels were made possible by much of the land belonging to the Crown. Not all these enterprises succeeded. In 1616 James I entered into an agreement with local landowners to drain King's Sedgemoor, the landowners undertaking to carry out the work. Nothing came of it. An attempt under Charles I failed, but later in his reign Alder Moor in the Brue Valley was drained and the bogland divided into fields in the ancient manner by dykes and ditches.

In contrast to the fluctuating fortunes of Somerset, so much of which was liable to flood in winter – hence its name 'the land of the summer dwellers' – the Dorset Vales were green and well drained all the year round. Consequently pastoral farming in Dorset has enjoyed security both 'up and along', as the local phrase has it, producing the continuity of life-styles and individuality in local character that are so marked as idiosyncrasies of personality in Hardy's most dramatic scenes, enabling the young to comment on situations of youth with the apparent experience of age. Despite the landscape contrasts between heath and heather, chalk and cheese, the Past is always to be sensed in the Present in Dorset. It is said that change came so slowly at Ashmore, that gem of a village, that a small tenant farmer in the reign of George III was still living the kind of life the villeins had lived under the Norman lords who added their names to so many groups of villages in Dorset: the four Peverells, the Fitzpains and the five Matravers (Maltravers).

One of the best places to see evidence of the open-field system in England, which continued under manorial control in Dorset into the nineteenth century, is in the parishes of Stratton and Grimstone

47

in the Frome Valley north-west of Dorchester, where the old arable land can be identified running down in tapering strips.

But the feudalism is not all of the same kind. The least disturbed is found around the Downs that thrust themselves into the county from Wiltshire in parishes which again bear significant names: Fifehead Neville, Sturminster Newton, Bishop's Caundle and Child Okeford. In other parts different traditions persist in groups dominated by ecclesiastical names, strongly monastic like Cerne Abbas, Winterborne Abbas and Abbas Combe. Gummershay Farm is identified with the dairy farm mentioned in a 1044 Saxon charter related to Wootton Abbas.* Doddings Farm, south of Bere Regis, was there at Domesday, and references to Chamberlayne's Farm, the two Stockley Farms, Philliol's Farm and Hyde Farm appear in twelfth- and thirteenth-century documents.

It is against this Norman and medieval background that the Dorset farmhouses rebuilt in the seventeenth century are to be seen and understood. Not all were rebuilt. One of the finest ancient manor houses surviving in England, surely, is the thirteenth-century Barnston Manor at Church Knowle, near Corfe Castle, built, like the magnificent cruciform church, of Purbeck limestone. And how better can we see at a glance the difference between Dorset and Somerset than by visualizing Corfe Castle, with the Purbeck Hills behind its ruins, and contrasting the scene with that of Dunster Castle, embowered in the greener hills of Somerset.

But the contrast must not be overstated. Dorset has other neighbours. On the east is Hampshire, and at East Tisted, four miles south of Jane Austen's Chawton, the cottages, almshouses and farmhouses are all in so civil and harmonious a composition with the squire's house that the scene is entirely one of benevolent lay patronage. Nor must we forget that when model villages came into vogue in the eighteenth century it was Dorset that produced the most picturesque in the street at Milton Abbas, planned in 1775 to rehouse families evicted when the earlier village was demolished to make way for the landscaping of the lord of the manor's parkland. Thatched cottages were neatly erected in pairs on either side of a wide road, with a chestnut tree planted between each. The scene

---

*Christopher Taylor, *Dorset* (The Making of the English Landscape Series, 1970)

Hayes Barton, East Budleigh, Devon: built with cob and thatch in traditional Devonshire fashion, Hayes Barton is the birthplace (1552) of Sir Walter Raleigh

Sanders, Lettaford, Devon: a granite-built longhouse on Dartmoor. Although now neatly slated, Sanders bears indications of once having been thatched. Inside, the house still retains its screens passage and, to the right of the front door, the original byre. (The house is a property of The Landmark Trust, which helps to preserve unusual buildings)

Edmeston, Modbury, Devon: representative of many a large farmhouse in south Devon. Of 1740 date and situated in a snug combe, the house is stone-built, slate-roofed, and possesses particularly well-proportioned windows

Quarleston Farm, Winterborne Stickland, Dorset: a very large, L-shaped house dating from the 15th century, of great architectural interest. Banded in stone and flint and showing signs of having once been rendered, the listed building deserved a better fate than the slow decay that overtook it in recent years

Hammoon Manor, Hammoon, Dorset: parts of the manor house date from
the 16th century. Interesting features include the classical porch
and extensive thatched roof

Woolbridge Manor, Wool, Dorset: a brick and stone building dating from
at least the 17th century, Woolbridge Manor was the home of a branch of
the famous Turberville family and the model for Wellbridge House in
Hardy's *Tess of the d'Urbervilles*

Little Toller Farm, Toller Fratrum, Dorset: dating from the 16th century. A stone monkey with a mirror may be discerned between the two central chimney stacks

Cottages at Bossington, Exmoor: cylindrical chimneys and sheltering porches are typical of the style throughout the Acland Exmoor estate, now the property of the National Trust

Roadside cottages at Minehead: cob cottages on the road to the open moor. The external chimney stack is typical and serves as a buttress; the rounded cornering is to reduce the risk of abrasion and crumbling in a region in which straight timber was scarce

Manor Farm, Bishopstone, Wiltshire: straw thatching in progress in the north-east of Wiltshire

Butler's Coombe Farm, Warminster, Wiltshire: a stone building parts of which date from Elizabethan times. To this a brick extension appears to have been added at a later date, yet both parts have rather puzzling lancet windows with hood moulds (At the time this photograph was taken the farm was soon to be broken up by construction of the Warminster bypass.)

Manor Farm, Tytherington, Wiltshire: A fine 18th-century farmhouse of dressed stone with a pedimented front door and an impressive pair of gate piers

The Dairy Farm, Weobley, Hereford & Worcester: many early farmhouses were built in cruck form but it is now comparatively rare to find a house where the crucks are still exposed externally. The farm dates back to the 16th century

Middle Bean Hall, Bradley, Hereford & Worcester: an example of the building style associated with the Welsh border. The use of black-painted timber in very regular and decorative form contrasts markedly with the plainer timber-framed buildings of other areas such as East Anglia and the south-east

Shell Manor, near Himbleton, Hereford & Worcester: a 15th and 16th century manor noteworthy for its solar wing, unusual porch, and massive chimney stacks the right-hand group of which bears a sundial

The Moat Farm, Dormston, Hereford & Worcester: note the tiled weatherings intended to direct rainwater clear of the walls and thus protect the fabric of the building. A tale is told of workmen who erased a date on the south-east gable. On returning from lunch they could not remember what had been there previously and so, rightly or wrongly, the house now bears the date 1663

must have been idyllic then (as it is serene now) but it was not always so. Milton Abbas had become so overcrowded in 1834 that many of the cottages had a family in every room.* And there was Tolpuddle!

On the other side of the picture there was the beauty of Dorset thatching continuing especially at Fontmell Magna, where modern work is 'signed' with the thatcher's insignia in the form of a bird or animal fashioned in straw.

Stone however is dominant in Dorset, but with weaker deposits on the fringes. On the chalk uplands of the north, pudding stone is combined with brick and flint to build farmhouses in the downland style common throughout the southern counties. Half Dorset is on chalk, and soil, as Wordsworth said, has 'a secret and mysterious soul'. It was Thomas Hardy's sensing of this that made the brooding heaths of Dorset the silent presence in his most dramatic soliloquies. It was the same sullen enmity in the soil that daunted generations of simple farmers who had only ox-drawn ploughs to break up the hard pan.

Elsewhere the soil of Dorset has a different and less mysterious secret soul. Dorset is a county with small streams coming together in wide valleys to allow villages to be formed at crossings. Beaminster, where four streams meet at the head of a valley, is a good example, and at Meerhay Farm there is a typical long, low, seventeenth-century Dorset farmhouse. In the Vale of Blackmore and on the green meadows along the feeder streams of the Stour, the Piddle and the Frome, cider-apple orchards and cornfields reflect a bountiful spirit of fertility that William Barnes celebrated in dialect verse which itself pays tribute to local vernacular.

The abundance of good stone has enabled masons in these valleys to build some of the sturdiest farmhouses in England, as well as drystone walls comparable with those of the Pennine dales. Every kind of farming seems to have been practised in some part of Dorset at one time or other, and an unusual variety has survived into the present. Faced with such variety, the inevitable question must be whether there is, in fact, a region that is distinctively typical of Dorset and could not be matched elsewhere. If I were

Dorset Nat. Hist. and Arch. Soc. Proc., LXXXIV (1962)

asked the question, I think I would answer that it starts in the Isle of Purbeck and from there extends in a broad swathe north-westward between Burton Bradstock and Dorchester towards the Devon and Somerset borders, particularly around Beaminster and the ridge where the Dorset sheep with black noses graze – or did before so much country stock-breeding got into such a muddle.

From Purbeck has come for centuries the 'marble' from which fonts have been carved and set up in churches all over England; from Portland the stone from which the finest towers have been built, even in places as far away from Dorset as Epping in Essex. In its home county this famous stone has been used for the humbler purpose of locally styled mullions, usually enclosing three lights under the heavy dripstones seen in so many of the best Dorset farmhouses. These, as well as the splendid porches, are as distinctively characteristic of Dorset as the similar but less elegant porches and mullioned windows of the Pennine dales are of Yorkshire. What matters is that, although local masons could do less with the grit and Carboniferous limestone of Yorkshire than with Portland stone, both harmonize perfectly with their respective landscapes – as, of course, all buildings do if they are built of local stone and designed in a spirit of good-neighbourliness.

A striking feature of Dorset farmhouses is the number that were built in the sixteenth century as manor-houses for the minor gentry – the local squires – who created the county's most typical landscapes and established its distinctive way of life. In the Isle of Purbeck the old buildings are entirely of stone – walls and roofs alike. This may appear to a casual observer too predominantly grey to be attractive until the sun breaks through, but the greyness is softened as the light brings colour to the lichens that flourish in the pure air of the south coast, while the roof slabs acquire family resemblances with the stone slabs of Horsham in Sussex and the Colly Westons of the Midlands.

The strength of Dorset stone, combined with the attachment of the people to established ways of life, has resulted in many farmhouses in the western vales evolving in recognizable stages in the way parish churches do. Woodcombe, at Wetherbury, south of Beaminster, was built as a single-storeyed longhouse in the seventeenth century and given an upper storey in the eighteenth as the cutting of the stones in the walling of this stage show. Camesworth in the same parish was built of rubble stone in the seventeenth century round a cob-walled dairy, which when a new dairy was built later was brought into use for cider-making. Other dairies built as separate units in the same parish are evidence of the prosperity that came to dairy farming in Dorset, as in so many other counties in pastoral country during the eighteenth century. Evidence of cob buildings that have been superseded by stone may be seen at Ford, Perhay and Whitehouse Farms, and at Denhay in the neighbouring parish of Symondsbury.

The explanation of this eighteenth-century prosperity in Dorset, particularly among counties in the South-West, is that dairy produce was then fetching good prices in the rapidly expanding London market. For the smaller farmers the cost of transporting produce to London in the canvas-canopied wagons of the period was heavy, since the journey from Bridport, for example, took four days. The more substantial farmers of Burton Bradstock and other good farming districts, however, were able to get their 'tubs of very prime salt butter' and hard cheeses weighing as much as 100 lbs shipped from Bridport.*

Blackmore Vale was Hardy's 'Vale of Little Dairies', with farmhouses standing back from the main road, as they still do. The surrounding pastures remain as green as they were in his day. The difference, alas, is that milking by machine has reduced the number of farmworkers growing their vegetables in cottage gardens.

For the true feel of farm life in the sheep country of southern England, there is no writer to touch Hardy, and his personal sensitivity to its character is shown in the adoption of the ancient name of Wessex for the countryside he peopled. We may think of the sheep-shearing in Bathsheba's great barn, with its 'dusky filmed chestnut roof, braced and tied in by hugh collars, curves and diagonals ... Along each wall was a range of striding buttresses, throwing deep shadows on the spaces between them.' The model for Bathsheba's farmhouse was Waterston Manor, near Puddletown.

Every writer on Dorset finds curious instances of the traditional

*Barbara Kerr, *Bound to the Soil*, John Baker, 1968

involvement of landowners with their tenant farmers. Arthur Young in his 1771 *Farmer's Tour* comments on the odd system found in the Dorset Vales, and to a lesser degree in neighbouring counties, of cows being hired out by the larger farmers to dairymen at prices varying according to the estimated yield of each beast. These cows were fed and foddered by the farmer on his land, while the dairyman was provided with a farmhouse and the keep of a mare to carry his butter to market. The mare was expected to produce a foal a year, and the dairyman could keep as many pigs and poultry as he wished.

In spite of this concentration on cattle, there was never a Dorset breed of cow. Even Lord Digby's herd at Sherborne was of Devon reds, the breed that was then practically universal in Dorset. The sheep-masters were more enterprising. Humphry Sturt, MP for Dorset, who owned large estates at Critchell, and William Frampton, who had several new farmhouses built with modern outbuildings on his estate between Moreton and Dorchester, were landowners, who in the late eighteenth and early nineteenth centuries cleared vast areas of unproductive heathland by burning and later manuring to introduce root crops in the way 'Turnip' Townshend did in Norfolk.* They represent the struggle with the Heath dramatized by Hardy, which was in fact the background of often valiant efforts made during the eighteenth and nineteenth centuries to liberate from medieval customs those who got their living from stubborn soil.

Blackmore Vale is on limestone and greensand sheltered by chalk hills. West of this chalk is a belt of Kimmeridge clay and a different kind of landscape. The farms are less compact, and as one allows the various Dorset landscapes to glide through the mind, it becomes apparent that too many geological bands are drawn together for the different styles of farmhouses to be summarized in a few pages. The great thing to be said about them is that all have the charm and quality of being built of local materials: stone from quarries in the hills, flint from chalk along the Wiltshire border, cob from clay dug in the vales, and thatch from their crops.

Such attempts at description can achieve little, since every Dorset

Dorset, Christopher Taylor (The Making of the English Landscape) 1970

mood and every labour of the months is re-created somewhere in
Hardy, from the first signs of life's renewal in Spring to nostalgic
farmhouse fireside scenes in winter, of which the finest, surely, is
the one in *The Return of the Native*, which is Dorset to the last
syllable:

The dining-room or hall, which they occupied at this time of year in
preference to the parlour, because of its large hearth, constructed for
turf fires ... was furnished, like every farmhouse of the period, with a
settle, which is the necessary supplement to a fire so open that nothing
less than a strong breeze will carry up the smoke. It is, to the hearths of
old-fashion cavernous fireplaces, what the east belt of trees is to the
exposed country estate, or the north wall of the garden. Outside the
settle candles gutter, locks of hair wave, young women shiver, and old
men sneeze. Not a symptom of a draught disturbs the air; the sitters'
backs are as warm as their faces, and songs and old tales are drawn
from the occupants by the comfortable heat, like fruit from
melon-plants in a frame.

3. West Midlands and Welsh Border

Cruck cottage, Stanway, Gloucestershire

Permanent building in timber began with the discovery of what could be done by splitting the trunks of wind-bent trees down the middle and opening out the base to form a sort of Gothic arch. When two or more of these were set upright in a row, they could be tied with withies to poles laid along them horizontally to form a frame capable of carrying a thatched roof. Stated in that crude way, we may wonder how so primitive a form of building came to be used universally until we see that it was based on the same principle as the boat, which would be a principle ingrained in Saxon carpenters using inverted boats for shelter after landing in them from the creeks and rivers of lowland England. They would soon learn that the strength of these cruck buildings, as they were called, was in having the grain running through the entire length, and for this there is no wood to surpass English oak.

Cruck-framed houses, like those built of cob, were originally single-storeyed. The first refinement would be to taper the apex to get a neat fit at the ridge, and to build the feet securely into a cill, leaving the broadest part at the eaves, which is where the main weight of the thatch would fall and where the rain could be carried off it. The next stage would come with the discovery of how easily tie beams could be introduced half way up the crucks for the insertion of balks, either to support sleeping-quarters or for storage. Then would come the idea of building a wall from the ground on which the crucks could be raised to provide more headroom for rooms on the upper floor and to prevent rot from the ground. Primitive forms of cruck framing come to light from time to time in the North of England when old houses are being demolished, and when old timbers that have been concealed by stone fall out. In the West Midlands, where timber was abundant in the forests of the Welsh Marches, cruck gables of great strength were common, and many of these are still fully exposed in village houses in Herefordshire and around Much Wenlock in Shropshire, to name only two regions in this well-wooded countryside. There is a particularly fine one at Weobley, with an outer frame to carry the roof at a still higher level. The whole village of Weobley is a ready-made museum of timber-framed buildings.

As the crucks carried the entire weight of the roof, the walls between them were free-standing. So when timber-framed buildings were fully developed on the cruck system, all the paraphernalia of wall-plates, collar beams, queen and king posts and clever jointing could be contrived for the adornment of houses on manor farms. This became especially notable in the West Midlands because Celtic influence is strong there, and the Celt is often given to showing off. Many of the cleverest devices were derived from adaptations of designs by Crown carpenters, who built lodges in the Royal Forests of the Marches. That so much local work has survived is due to the invariable custom of building in oak.

There is a common belief that timber was stouter in the West

Midlands than elsewhere. Whether that is capable of proof may be doubted, since the forests of the South-East were ravaged by iron-smelters before the Midlands became 'Black Country'. What is not in doubt is that the timber-framed houses of the West Midlands were far more elaborate in style, and heavier in construction, than anything built in Kent during the reigns of Elizabeth and James I. The West Midland enthusiasm for lozenges and similar conventional designs would have been thought ostentatious in the South-East. Even the simpler designs found in whole villages like Eardisland, Orleton, Pembridge and Weobley cannot be matched in the ancient forest counties of Essex, Kent and Sussex. Clearly they were derived from different traditions: Continental in the South-East, Welsh in the West.

The boldness that found expression in carved braces and diagonal struts continued northward into Cheshire and Lancashire, producing tall bay windows carried up through two and even three storeys in hexagonal and octagonal protuberances, for which the only logical explanation would be to provide more light to relieve the gloom of excessively heavily timbered halls, with ceilings blackened with smoke from fires kept blazing throughout both summer and winter to reduce damp.

Halls of this type are now showpieces and well known by name to most people, but by the end of the fifteenth century yeomen as well as Court favourites and ecclesiastical dignitaries were living in houses as heavily timbered, if smaller. In these we find a feature that became common in the 'statesmen's houses' of Cumbria: a fixed screen on the door side of the hearth to baffle the draught. In the Midlands it was called either a speer or a spur, and its introduction so early is evidence of open fires being positioned at one end of the hall when in other parts of the country they were still in the middle. No doubt the major factor in the resiting of the open fire was the constancy in direction of prevailing winds. In the North and West of England the hills rise steeply on one, two and sometimes even three sides of an isolated farmhouse, giving protection from all the winds except the one which sweeps up the valley. Where the direction of the wind could be anticipated, there was no need to provide for the smoke to escape from an opening in the middle of the roof. In fact, that was the worst place for it,

Little Moreton Hall, Cheshire

because the biggest nuisance was down-draughts, which a vent in
the ridge was liable to catch. So a hole in the form of an inverted V
was left at the apex of the gable away from the wind.

The most typically local in style of the half-timbered farmhouses
of the West Midlands date from the last quarter of the sixteenth
and the first quarter of the seventeenth centuries, which is
approximately a hundred years later than those in Kent and Sussex.
The best known is Little Moreton Hall in Cheshire, which grew in
stages during the sixteenth century to accommodate succeeding
generations of the family. The hall and gateway are dated *c.*1520.
The porch and parlour were added about 1560 and are the work of
Richard Dale, an eminent master carpenter. Twenty years later the
Long Gallery was built, and with that the ambitions of the family
seem to have been fully realized.

Like other homes of long-established Cheshire families, Little
Moreton continued to be both a manor-house and a farmhouse in
the fullest sense of each word until the last of the Moreton heirs

Huddington Court, Worcestershire

conveyed it to the National Trust in 1938. Its importance is that we have in it the culmination of local style, with the magnificently timbered hall behind an imposing gatehouse giving access across a moat. The farm buildings are at the rear.

When the massive timbers of these Cheshire manor-houses had been assembled on the ground and jointed, they were winched into position and pegged. The panels were then filled with wattle and daub by plasterers so skilled that the City companies of Chester included Daubers. This suggests that here we have a factor in the evolution of West Midlands farmhouses not encountered to the same degree in the southern counties at this date. These elaborately styled country houses were obviously being built by city craftsmen who were members of guilds under the patronage of wealthy merchants. That is why Chester and Shrewsbury are the English showpieces for such houses. This continued development of timber-framed manor- and farmhouses in the West so long after brick had come into favour for dwellings of this status in the East had two major causes: the availability of timber in the old Royal Forests into the seventeenth century and the weight of Kerridge stone roofs, so strongly favoured.

A striking feature of the most typical timber-framed farmhouses in the West Midlands is that the normal extension of the hall-house by adding wings to it seems to have stopped short after only one had been built. This results in a large proportion of Midland farmhouses being L-shaped, with a chimney-stack at the axis. One of the most striking is Huddington Court in Worcestershire. Another local feature is the number of front walls carried up through the eaves into roof gables, as at Clear Brook Farm, Pembridge, Herefordshire, which has good decorative work on the gables. This West Midlands characteristic is Welsh in origin. At Orleton Manor House, five miles north of Leominster, a fine oriel window above the porch is obviously Welsh in style. There is also elaborate surface treatment at Luntley Court (1673), near Dilwyn, between Leominster and Weobley.

In every part of Herefordshire we see evidence of the availability of timber long after it had become scarce in the South-East of England, and Herefordshire was famous for its schools of carpentry in the Middle Ages.* John Abel, the greatest of all the post-medieval architects in timber, was a Herefordshire man. At the same time we must acknowledge that ecclesiastical explanations are not required to account for the wide cross-passages at Lower Jury Farm, Abbey Dore, which is reminiscent of Devon and no doubt originated in use by wide-horned oxen.

There was a vigorous period of rebuilding all along the Welsh border from 1660 to 1725, and in no other part of England are so many local-style buildings so well preserved. Hereford and Worcester have much in common and are now united for purposes of local government. Both came early into association with Kent for fruit marketing. The Vale of Evesham challenges the south-eastern county for the title 'Garden of England', while Herefordshire challenges it on the superior quality claimed for its hops, though certainly not on the quantity grown. Two-thirds of the hops grown in England still come from Kent. Hop-growing must have been well established in Herefordshire at the end of the seventeenth century, when Celia Fiennes, after standing on the top of the Malvern Hills, wrote: 'On the other side is Herefordshire, which

*Sir William Addison, *Local Styles of the English Parish Church*, B.T. Batsford, 1982

appears to be a county of Gardens and Orchards, the whole Country being full of fruit trees etc, it looks like nothing else, the apple, pear trees etc. are so thick even in their corn fields and hedgerows.'

Whether in eastern or western England, the luxuriant growth of hops along labyrinthian aisles and avenues produces annually an outdoor scene that no other English crop can rival. The nearest equivalents are the orchards which are seen at their best in Kent and Worcestershire, but these lack the distinctive architecture of the hop kilns called oast houses, which did not reach the West Midlands until the present century. The explanation of this late introduction was purely economic. As hops were produced in smaller quantities here than in Kent, and special buildings for drying them were required for only two months in the year, a room in the farmhouse was adapted for storage – usually the one already in use as dairy or buttery; but in older farmhouses treading-holes can be identified, below which canvas bags were hung to receive the trodden hops. In larger farms granaries would be used to serve the second purpose.

The hop-pickers were in three distinctive groups: Welsh, Midlanders and gipsies. As the three did not mix, farmers had to make their choice and stick to it, building ranges of hostels round their farmyards for Midlanders, providing transport for Welsh and laying out camping grounds for gipsies. Terrible fights would break out in the alehouses between rival pickers, leading to such signs as 'No Gipsies' being prominantly displayed on forecourts. Some of the smaller alehouses, glad of any business they could get, put out trestle tables and forms for gipsies, serving drink on those to gipsies only during the hop-picking season. This continued until alternative methods of hop-picking were introduced.

It was the same Arcadian scene in the orchards, where apples for cider took the place of hops for beer, and where Giles Winterborne in Hardy's *The Woodlanders*, 'looked and smelt like Autumn's very brother, his face being sunburned to wheat-colour, his eyes blue as corn-flowers, his sleeves and leggings dyed with fruit-stains, his hands clammy with the sweet juice of apples, his hat sprinkled with pips, and everywhere about him that atmosphere of cider which at its first return each season has such an indescribable fascination for those who have been born and bred among the orchards'. For cider-making the identifiable building was a circular mill in which a horse-driven wheel of stone crushed the fruit in a trough.

Nearly every Herefordshire farm has its orchard, and scores of them must have cider mills. In such a county it is not surprising that the county town should be unsurpassed as a market town as well as being the least spoilt of county towns in the West of England. In fact, three-quarters of Herefordshire is still under grass, and grass that somehow always looked greener and sweeter than that in any other county – hence the magnificent red cattle, with white faces and dewlaps, that grow fat on it. Although Herefordshire farmers are fond of claiming that they would rather live rich than die rich, the truth is that they make a good job of doing both.

As elsewhere, mechanical harvesting has taken much of the colour out of the autumn scene, and technology has reduced much of the acreage of land under hops. The effect of this was already becoming apparent in the 1760s and 1770s when the acreage under hops fell by approximately fifteen per cent during successive years in which the consumption of beer was increasing by a percentage greater than that. Hops are grown for what are scientifically called the 'alpha resins', the ingredient that gives beer the 'bitter' taste which distinguishes it from ale. In the old days brewers were supposed to buy their hops on personal assessment – made by the appearance, rub and smell of their quality. Now brewers put their money on the results of scientific research on these 'alpha resins' being carried out at Wye College in Kent and the Rosemaund Experimental Husbandry Farm in Herefordshire.

Historically, Herefordshire is not a county of large farms. The number of 'cote' names in the West Midlands, and especially in the Cotswolds, indicates that this was smallholding country in the Middle Ages. The word 'cote' means 'cot' or cottage, although there are instances where it is derived from the Old English *cotlif*, signifying a manor or a 'court'. This smallholdings tradition was revived in the Vale of Evesham for cultivating the black soil under the great scarp of Broadway Hill in the middle of the nineteenth century, when several big farms in the Vale came into the market. Instead of being sold as single units, they were broken up for sale to the labourers who had worked them. The idea, called 'the Evesham

Custom', was then seized upon as a means of bringing the region into more intensive cultivation. Worcestershire County Council bought a number of the farms and split them up into hundreds of smallholdings to be cultivated for fruit and garden produce. Each had a small house built on it, and facilities were provided for irrigating the plots and washing vegetables. Set between the distinctively styled Cotswold villages and the Georgian town of Pershore, these new houses added nothing to the architectural attraction of the Vale, but anyone who travels through the Evesham orchards when the trees are in blossom, or when the fruits are ripe and stalls along the roadside are laden with apples, plums and peaches, cannot fail to rejoice in the cheerfulness and enterprise of the present-day Evesham fruit-gardeners who continue to contribute so much life and colour to the Vale through the restoration a century ago of an ancient smallholding custom.

The reference to apples recalls John Drinkwater's lines:

At the top of the house the apples are laid in rows,
   And the skylight lets the moonlight in ...
They are lying in rows there, under the gloomy beams;
   On the sagging floor.

In these fruit-growing counties farmhouses did have rooms under the rafters, with floors boarded for the fruit to be laid out on to ripen. They were spread out in this way to prevent rotten apples touching their wholesome neighbours and infecting them as they did when stored in barrels.

In Shropshire we turn again to local writers for the feel of farm life and descriptions of buildings. We get both in the novels of Mary Webb, particularly in the best-known of them, *Precious Bane*, where we have a description of a typical Shropshire farmhouse, with 'attic window in the big gable, and the roof on one side went down to the ground, with a tall chimney standing up above the roof tree ... There was a great wooden bolt on the door ... All the beams and rafters were oak, and the floor went up and down like stormy water. The apples and pears had their places [on the floor] all round the room.' An itinerant weaver visited at regular intervals, working at a loom in the attic, where there was a bed for him to sleep in, 'since the work for him might keep him busy for two or three days'.

62

This last note is a reminder of something that is now almost forgotten: the weaving room. Commodious farmhouses have their sewing-room, but early this century farmhouses still had first-floor rooms called weaving-rooms, from the time when they had been used either by itinerant or in Lancashire by hand-loom weavers. These itinerant weavers were succeeded by Scottish drapers, who also called at regular intervals and took measurements for new garments to be delivered on the next visit.

But the West Midlands are predominantly pastoral, giving their names to famous cheeses. A fine description of a Midland dairy comes from George Eliot in *Adam Bede*: 'The dairy was certainly worth looking at ... such colours, such coolness, such purity, such fresh fragrance of new-pressed cheese, of farm butter, of wooden vessels perpetually bathed in pure water; such soft colouring of red earthenware and creamy surfaces, brown wood and polished tin, grey limestone and rich orange-red rust on the iron weights and hooks and hinges.'

Before the eighteenth century, English cheeses were considered inferior to European. It was said of Suffolk cheese that, 'Pigs grunt at it, dogs bark at it, but none dare bite it.' The monks of Battle Abbey in Kent produced cheese from the milk of ewes that grazed on Romney Marshes. The West Midlands cheeses were made from cows' milk, yet made slow progress. Marketing seems to have been the early problem with Cheddar, now the most popular English cheese. Throughout the eighteenth century it was classed with Gloucester, although so much in demand at the end of the century that large Cheddar cheeses were being sold in London as Double-Gloucester. A definite formula for its manufacture was not issued until 1856.

Gloucester cheese, with its waxlike texture derived from strict adherence to a method of production established early, was on stronger ground. Stilton, the luxury cheese originally made of cream, later of full milk (although now, like Cheddar and Gloucester, made in more than half a dozen Midlands counties), has at least always known how it got its name. It was first made early in the eighteenth century by Mrs Paulet of Wymondham, near Melton Mowbray, who sold it to Cooper Thornhill, who kept the Bell at Stilton, with whose customers it was so popular that quality cheese-making became a local industry over a wide area.

Warwickshire, at the heart of the Midlands, has inevitably become more heavily industrialized than its neighbours to the west, but its association with Shakespeare has kept it tourist-conscious, and old farmhouses are maintained in the traditional black-and-white style, popularly known as 'magpie', which has come to be regarded as the 'correct' style for timber-framed buildings everywhere, which it is not.

The tarring of timbers in the West was introduced to safeguard them from the weather in regions of high rainfall. A fine example of the Warwickshire style is carefully conserved at Wilmcote, four miles north-west of Stratford-on-Avon, in the reputed home of Mary Arden, Shakespeare's mother, which is in every respect a typical farmhouse, with an enormous fireplace, flagged floors etc. It is now the property of the Shakespeare Birthday Thrust and open to visitors.

Brick took over from timber for building farmhouses in the West Midlands generally in the eighteenth century. In Warwickshire whole villages are built of it, and brick invaded even stone-proud Gloucestershire at Preston-upon-Stour. In most small towns and villages brick and black-and-white half-timbering have settled down well together. Towns like Upton-on-Severn derive their character from the mingling, as do Evesham, Tewkesbury and Ledbury now, while Pershore owes everything architecturally to its Georgian brick and eighteenth-century ironwork. But brick-building styles were never completely vernacular. Their special importance in the Midlands is that they came as the result of the great enclosures made in the Midlands counties, resulting in village farmhouses being converted into cottages as new farmhouses were built in the middle of fields that had recently been commons, with farm buildings round a courtyard behind them, reminiscent of the lay-out of smaller Roman villas of fifteen hundred years earlier in Gloucestershire.

For these new buildings bricks could be brought in to meet every planning requirement, and multiples of brick sizes determined the size, shape and symmetry appropriate for every need. The problem of where to place the chimney-stack solved itself. It was no longer necessary to place it where it would best stabilize the framework of the house. Good proportions took care of strains and stresses. Elegance entered into the reckoning, and styles were chosen from pattern-books with little regard to local material or tradition.

It is estimated that in Shropshire, over the period of thirty years 1770-1800, the number of farms diminished by one-third, and that by 1803 throughout the county the size of farms had increased enormously as the result of two, three or even four farms being consolidated into one.* This meant that the average farmer was a man of substance to a degree not known in most parts of the Midlands previously. He became a businessman with his eye on the expanding Midlands market for farm produce, and larger kitchens, milk-houses and brewhouses were built onto the rear of the new farmhouses – many of which were called Newhouse Farm – than had ever been seen in the Midlands before. Provision was made in the lofts for storing fruit, butter, cheese and hops, which showed that, despite aggrandizement, the basic character of Midlands farming was preserved.

*Trevor Rowley, *The Shropshire Landscape*, p.148

4. *East Anglian Flint and Brick*

Flint and brick, East Anglia

This is one part of England in which climate, soil and weather have conspired to produce ideal conditions for ripening grain. So Norfolk farmers are able to boast of their ability to supply in abundance what were once considered the three staple items of a healthy diet, bread, beef and beer. The light soils produce barley for the brewer, the heavy wheat for the baker, while the marshes fatten bullocks for the butcher. West of Norfolk are the East Anglian fens, where since the seventeenth-century, when drainage schemes were finally introduced successfully by Dutch engineers, the black soil produces incomparably rich crops.

The farmhouses of the region may be less interesting architecturally than the churches, but they fascinated artists of the stature of Constable and members of the Norwich school by the way their surfaces reflect the marvellous East Anglian light. There are no skies in England like those of East Anglia, where the slight tilt of the landscape to the east results in every detail being clearly defined as the light relates the most commonplace objects to the life about it, which is farm and sporting life.

Dutch, Flemish and French Huguenot influences can be deciphered in the farmhouses and ancillary buildings of every East Anglian village and market town where refugees from religious persecution on the Continent settled, and in the ports, where Dutch surnames bear testimony to the traders who brought in tiles from Holland.

The history of East Anglian vernacular starts with flint. Geologists tell us that the white encrusted nodules that lie on the surface of every ploughed field on chalk have been transported immense distances since they broke away from their parent rock in the Ice Age. They are now the improbable material from which the most characteristic farmhouses and cottages are built. Without documentary evidence, the dating of flint buildings is notoriously difficult. When firmly embedded in mortar, flint walls may remain unchanged for centuries. We know this from fragments excavated from Saxon and Roman sites. The earliest use of flint in surviving buildings above the surface of the land is probably in the cobble stone walls in the north of Norfolk. Their use is more widespread in defensive and ecclesiastical architecture, but in domestic architecture the main concentration is in buildings dating from the end of the fourteenth century between Wells and Sheringham.

Reliable dating of flint farmhouses starts when they can be related to monastic remains, and it is interesting to note that the knapped flints used in minor domestic buildings in East Anglia, in contrast to those found on the North and South Downs, are usually inferior to the flints used in building churches. It seems reasonable to infer from this that most of the material used for the houses had been discarded by the masons who built the churches. However, as on the chalk south of the Thames, East Anglia had many small abbeys and priories, which after the Dissolution would serve as quarries for farm buildings. Walsingham, Lynn, Bromholm and Castle Acre all grew rich from the offerings of pilgrims.

Where domestic architecture in East Anglia scores over ecclesiastical is in rich variety of material. Starting from the north-west, there is carstone, a soft coarse-grained sandstone coloured brown by oxide of iron, which may be seen in the cliffs at Hunstanton and which has been quarried at Snettisham for nearly a thousand years. The manor house there and several houses built on the royal estate at Sandringham in traditional style show how well modern buildings in this material can harmonize with the old.

Norfolk is not a well-wooded county when compared with Suffolk or mid-Essex, so it is not eminent for timber-framed buildings. It has, however, an outstanding example which could not have been built in any other county, in the Old Hall Farmhouse, Talcolneston, which has a unique three-storeyed porch projecting from the front elevation, and crow-stepped gables that are typically Norfolk in style. There is so much East Anglian independence of character in the whole of this building that, however incongruous some of the features may be, the end product is both dignified and impressive. Perhaps the most extraordinary feature is a centrally placed projecting wing at the rear, with upper floors built in diminishing stages like West Midland belltowers. They are all plastered and heavily timbered, with Tudor windows. The same Norfolk independence of mind has resulted in distinctively styled farmhouses being built in wattle-and-daub, clunch and clay-lump in the south, and brick in the east, all used with virtuosity as well as skill.

Flint farmhouses are best seen on the Raynham estate, especially at East Raynham. But the finest is the Elizabethan Old Hall Farm at Toftrees, south of Fakenham, which conforms with the E-shaped Elizabethan plan except that it is built with flint facing instead of the usual East Anglian brick. A custom to be noted in most of the sturdy farmhouses in east Norfolk and along the Fenland roads is that they are built like those we noted in the West Country, at right-angles to the highway.

In tracing the evolution of these forthright Norfolk farmhouses, it is often useful to be on the lookout for development in stages from flint, through clay-lump (clay-bats) or clunch to brick. One of the most fascinating instances of this is the Old Manor Farm at Northwold, which was built in the fifteenth century as a parsonage house when the parson farmed his glebe and was as earthy-minded as any of his parishioners. The west wing is of clunch, the main structure of flint and T-shaped, with a fine brick gable to the south and original hood moulds to the Tudor windows, which have been replaced in the two lower storeys with early eighteenth-century windows.

The date of the introduction – or reintroduction – of brickmaking in the eastern counties is a subject for experts. Scores of Essex and East Anglian churches have 'Roman brick' in their walls. Most of them are near enough to sites of Roman occupation to make it reasonable to assume that the implied dating is accurate. The Saxons may have found all they required for their modest purposes in abandoned Roman buildings, but whether it is safe to infer that brickmaking ceased entirely after the withdrawal of the legions in the fourth century may be open to question. Since Essex and East Anglia have clays similar to those found in Flanders, this may be a subject for new research to be undertaken to ascertain whether the earliest post-Roman bricks were imported or made locally. We are fortunate in having Mr Warwick Rodwell working at present on the archaeology of Essex churches.

In the present state of knowledge it is sufficient to be able to claim that the use of brick with flint, which is so attractive a feature of the buildings in north Essex and East Anglia, began about the end of the twelfth century. We find it in the Abbot's Lodging at Little Coggeshall in Essex, which experts now date *c.*1190, in the form usually referred to as tiles. They are rough in texture and flat, measure thirteen inches by six and are about two inches thick. Bricks in the Gatehouse at Waltham Abbey, *c.*1370, are fifteen inches long. So the question is sometimes posed as to when a tile starts to be a brick! In fact, the Norman French word *briche*, variously spelt *brik, bricke, brike* and *bryk*, did not come into use in England until late in the fourteenth century, although smaller 'bricks' were used in the thirteenth, most notably at Little Wenham Hall in Suffolk, *c.*1280, where they measure nine inches by $4\frac{1}{2}$, are two inches thick and are thus only marginally different from the standard size today.

Bricks were imported in ships of the Hanseatic League, a powerful commercial combine established in the Low Countries and north Germany, and landed at eastern ports in the middle of the thirteenth century. The same ships and the same ports received immigrant brickmakers who would not only lay bricks but teach the English how to lay them. This means that, if the art of brickmaking had been lost after the Roman withdrawal, it was revived in eastern England in the second half of the thirteenth century and so now has seven hundred years of history behind it. It seems reasonable to suppose that the adoption of the standard size of brick was due to its being the most convenient size for the bricklayer to handle. If this is accepted, the fact that medieval bricks are thinner than modern would be explained by the medieval hand, as shown in suits of armour, being smaller than ours.

Early bricks made in England were dark red in colour, indicating a high concentration of oxide of iron in the brick-earth from which the clay had been dug. When fully developed, the brickmaking industry was able to utilize local clay to bring this manufactured product into as close a relationship with the earth it came from as stone had always had. For example, the white bricks associated with Suffolk came from brick-earth in which lime predominates, whereas on the edge of the Fens the chalk is less evident in the clay, and the brick weathers to the yellow colour seen in all the villages eastwards of the Wash and in the Norfolk villages between King's Lynn and Thetford. Some of the seventeenth-century farmhouses in the region are built of it.

The fashion for building in brick was started by the rich wool merchants who brought back bricks as ballast in the ships which exported wool to the Low Countries. Royal patronage played a part, which at least partly explains why the attractive small bricks that have weathered so warmly are usually referred to as Tudor. It must have been the wealth of East Anglia, together with the favours bestowed on the region by Tudor sovereigns, that led to the use of brick in building the ostentatiously ornate chimneystacks of Elizabethan manor-houses, copied by the yeoman who built such splendid farmhouses towards the end of Elizabeth I's reign and continued to build them throughout that of James I. Such chimneystacks became so widespread that William Harrison of Radwinter, in his *Description of England*, reported that his elderly parishioners marvelled to 'see multitudes of brick chimneys lately erected', but added wryly: 'Now we have many chimneys, and yet our tenderlings complain of rheums, catarrhs and poses.'*

*poses – colds in the head

The first brick houses built in East Anglia were thoroughly English in style – Little Wenham Hall in Suffolk is the supreme example. The influence of Flemish architects is seen at Little Hautbois Hall, near Downham Market in Norfolk, and from the time of its building Continental influences provide a running commentary, particularly evident in the development in styles of chimneystacks and fireplaces in manor-houses, followed by those in other farmhouses. Little Hautbois Hall has special features, but it can be seen from the outside to have two chimneystacks in the middle of the building, one for the hall, the other for the parlour. While providing stability for the structure, the greater wealth of Norfolk landowners and farmers enabled these massive chimney-breasts to be developed for other purposes. In some they were thick enough to support a staircase constructed to run up from the hall opposite the main entrance.

With the introduction of brick, it was no longer necessary for thatched roofs to be hipped to prevent the wind getting under them at the eaves. In Norfolk the ferocity of the winds blowing in from the North Sea was early dealt with ingeniously by building houses with gable ends rising above the ridge and rafters so that they could grip the thatch between them. Strong corbels were built along the eaves for the same reason. These gables and corbels now appear as the only decorative features on farmhouses that are otherwise completely plain. Originally their function was entirely utilitarian. In Norfolk end gables are by no means always of brick. They are often of flint, at least in part, even if the front is entirely of brick. Modifications of these plain East Anglian styles are invariably due to Continental, usually Dutch, influence; but however plain East Anglian farmhouses may be, they never fail to please the eye by their simplicity and good proportions.

In the old manor-houses that retain their farms, the corbelling may project five or six inches from the eaves and carry ornaments, as they do at Church Farm, Great Hautbois, north-west of Broadland, and at Priory Farm, Bedingham, near Bungay on the Waveney, which has three fine chimneystacks and is clearly a farmhouse with a history. Old Hall Farm at Bedingham has curved gables over the porch and the principal window as well as at the ends of the building. These curvilinear gables, called 'Dutch gables', are usually seventeenth-century but where windows have them they are eighteenth. Walnut Farmhouse and Hall Common Farmhouse at Ludham – the Broadland village that takes most pride in its curvilinear brickwork – have these Jacobean style Dutch gables but with Georgian windows.

Farmhouses in the north of the county and along the Fenland border are plain and serviceable buildings that express in flint and brick the forthright character of the East Anglian yeoman represented by Old Strowd of Norfolk in *The Blind Beggar of Bethnal Green*, who despised his son's pretence of being a gentleman:

> Come off with this trash,
> This bought gentility, that sits on thee
> Like peacock's feathers cock't upon a raven.

A yeoman's estate had been good enough for the father and should satisfy the son:

> I am as proud,
> And think myself as gallant in this gray,
> Having my table furnished with good beef.
> Norfolk temes bread and country home-bred drink,
> As he that goeth in rattling taffety.
> Let gentlemen go gallant, what care I.
> I was a yeoman born, and so I'll die.

That Old Strowd was so contented with his lot was rooted in his pride in what the yeomen of East Anglia had done with the soil they tilled despite the enmity of the winds that blew in from the North Sea. Their drink was from barley grown on the light soil, their flour from wheat grown on the clay in such abundance that the coarser bran, still customary for baking bread elsewhere, had been withdrawn in Norfolk from the family table and fed to beasts.

The material of which the farmhouses on the borders of Cambridgeshire and in the Isle of Ely were built has already been described in Chapter 1, 'Cob and Thatch'. In the east of the county, trade with the Low Countries resulted in brick being mixed with flint, and tile replacing thatch in the seventeenth-century rebuilding boom. All along the east coast as far as Cleveland in the north tiles were – and still are – of the wavy type called pantiles: curved tiles laid to form channels that allow the rainwater to run down the roof into the troughs along the eaves. Since the eighteenth century these have been made locally in many parts. I don't know how strong the evidence for it is, but Daniel Defoe is reputed to have introduced their manufacture in England at the works he established at Tilbury in Essex in a venture which failed. Others must have come in about the same time to have made their adoption so widespread. As the wind is just as liable to lift pantiles as to lift thatch, gable ends continued to be parapeted until barge-boards were imported in quantity and given a name which must be a corruption of 'vergeboard'. So long as the ends of the tiles were packed with a cement filling, the barge-boards served the same purpose as parapets. At the same time local conservatism demanded that the roofs should continue to be highpitched.

Brick building started so early in East Anglia that the range of the varieties used is too wide to describe here. It must be borne in mind that before the invention of the Hoffman Kiln in 1858 bricks continued to be made by hand. The convenience of handling dictated the size during most of the period, but when in 1784 a tax was imposed on their manufacture without specifying size, there was a tendency to make large, uninteresting bricks, many of which can still be seen in farm buildings and late eighteenth- and early nineteenth century bridges. It was a tax extremely difficult to enforce and was abolished in the middle of the nineteenth century. Despite the many dignified Georgian houses built during the period, it must be acknowledged that for brickwork the late eighteenth and early nineteenth centuries were not a good period.

The main general point to look out for in dating brickwork is the difference between English and Flemish bond. Until the end of the seventeenth-century bricks were usually laid in alternate courses of headers and stretchers, which meant that along one entire course the ends of the bricks faced the wall, along the next the sides. This was called English bond and was common form. But during the course of the century Flemish bond was introduced, in which headers and stretchers alternated in every course, and gradually this became practically universal. An attractive feature of East Anglian

73

Barn with Dutch gable, Norfolk

walling is the use of darker bricks for headers to produce a diaper design, a device derived from local knowledge of how different types of clay could be further varied in colour by using different firing methods. This was also applied to roofing tiles. In Norfolk the pantiles are usually glazed and dark in colour.

In the use of flint and brick in combination, the most interesting contrasts are between practices in Kent and East Anglia. Flint is common in the Isle of Thanet in Kent, and in fact in the downland villages of West Sussex as far as Chichester and the Hampshire border. In the counties south of the Thames there is flint and brick chequering but much less ingenuity than in East Anglia in overall designing, which may appear surprising since farmhouses built entirely of brick, or even with brick gables, are rare in either Kent or Sussex earlier than the eighteenth century. The most notable exceptions in the south-east, including Surrey, are Crossways Farm, Abinger Hammer (*c.*1610), Fulvers, Shere (*c.*1630) and Brook Place, Chobham (*c.*1630).

The greater influence of the Dutch in East Anglia accounts for much of the difference, particularly in the curvilinear gables. One of the best Dutch gables on a Norfolk farmhouse is at Kimberley, near Wymondham, but farmhouses with Dutch characteristics are found all over the county. There is an outstanding one at Ringstead on the Peddars Way east of Hunstanton, and many of the best are in the south, along the Waveney Valley. Barns, as memorials of medieval life, are less prominent than in the west of England, but two that must catch the eye are those at Waxham and Paston, and there is no more evocative record of farmhouse manorial life in the second half of the fifteenth century than the *Paston Letters*.

The eastern ports continued to bring in new settlers, who introduced Continental and Scandinavian crafts and skills into the towns. Of these, building styles are the ones that have most permanently influenced East Anglian vernacular. Mansard roofs, for example, came into fashion at the end of the sixteenth century as a simple means of gaining more space and light without imposing too much additional stress on exisiting walls. Improved methods of laying floor joists were adopted early. With the importation of soft woods at the ports from Scandinavia, all the joinery features of dwelling-houses, including door and window frames, staircases, skirtingboards and roof timbers, were transformed in the eighteenth century.

Unfortunately, these soft woods fail to harden as oak does. It was found that if they were to give reasonable service they must have a protective skin of paint, the best of which was lead oxide. So, with red brick walls and white painted woodwork, Norfolk farmhouses acquired the new look found throughout the Home Counties. Built with their backs to the farmyard, with large sash windows overlooking a countryside in process of being relandscaped by parliamentary enclosures, these eighteenth-century farmhouses reflected the vastly improved status of the tenant farmer as English agriculture moved into its Golden Age. Because enclosures were so widespread across the Midlands, these brightly coloured red-and-white Georgian farmhouses are associated chiefly with counties already described, but the most elegantly appointed and most graciously proportioned have always been in the eastern Home Counties and along the Thames Valley through Buckinghamshire.

Inevitably, East Anglia had its own attitude to what was happening all over southern England. In most counties it was a question of brick coming to terms with timber; in East Anglia brick had to come to terms with flint — flint from the soil and flint in the character of the men who worked it. Like Old Strowd, every East Anglican farmer and builder knew the worth of what he already had, so change was seldom revolutionary. In Norfolk it usually found expression in an expanded use either of flint in combination with brick or of brick in combination with flint. Neither was normally allowed to assert dominance. Brick, for example, might be used to frame panels of flint. The extending of brick lacing courses across the entire front of the house, with Dutch gables to add a flourish, was adopted in some places.

Weatherboarding, which Americans call clapboarding, became ornamental, as though to rival the 'Colonial style' houses in New England, which were themselves a development of the style taken across the Atlantic by the Pilgrim Fathers from East Anglia and Essex. In fact, the use of weatherboarding as well as flint goes back to the Anglo-Saxons in the south-eastern counties, with the difference that the early settlers sheathed their buildings with boards fixed vertically. Weatherboarding was with wedge-shaped boards laid horizontally so that each overlapped the one below it.

In the eighteenth century brick-nogging replaced wattle-and-daub for infilling panels in timber-framed buildings in eastern England, as it had done earlier in the West Midlands, but it was not entirely satisfactory. If the bricks were too heavy for the purpose, they caused the timber-framing to warp. And brick-nogging was less effective than wattle-and-daub in excluding draughts, since the bricks could not be sprung into the studs in the way the wattle panels had been. So weatherboarding established itself as the most popular form of wall cladding in East Anglia and Essex, where there is reason to think it was first used on windmills.

When we cross the Waveney into Suffolk, we enter a mellower countryside and one that is almost entirely the creation of farmers who took as much pride in their land as did Old Strowd of Norfolk or any yeoman of Kent. Cobbett found Suffolk farmers 'great boasters' but added, 'and I must say it is not without reason'. Not every county can show such breeds to its credit as the Suffolk Punch horse, the Red Poll cow and the Suffolk black-faced sheep. The handsome, sleek-coated chestnut horses seen today, tossing their heads with such pride in their strength and brisk movement, are very different from the animals described in the eighteenth century as 'half-horse, half-hog'. They are a magnificent achievement in being the only English carthorse that shows no trace of Spanish ancestry. The original stock probably came from Norway. The lack of feather on the legs make the breed peculiarly suitable for working on heavy Suffolk clay, and the low withers, thick neck and strong buttocks give it tremendous pulling power.

The success of Suffolk farmers in making the most of what Nature had given them to work with reflects their own native character, which is as hardy and mettlesome as that of their beautiful horses. And every characteristic is reflected in their farmhouses, especially in those in mid-Suffolk and the Stour Valley. My own experience is that it is difficult to fault a true East Anglian in anything he gives his mind to. The native wit and shrewdness of the race is reflected in the large number of East Anglian authors who figure in every Dictionary of Quotations – Bacon, of course, giving them a good start. They are masters of a terse, epigrammatic style that seems to have the bite of marshland air in it. Arthur Young, the agricultural surveyor, was outstanding for the vigour and vividness of his Reports, if inferior to William Marshall in perception. Neither he nor his forerunner as an East Anglian commentator, Tusser, farmed successfully. But they are not the first of whom it may be said: 'Those who can, do; those who can't, tell others what to do.'

So with an abundance of oak on its heavy clay, and with a race of men bred to take pride in their work, it is only to be expected that Suffolk should have produced some of the finest timber-framed farmhouses in England. In any contest for, say, the best twenty, Kent would probably win, but if the condition were attached that they must still be occupied by working farmers, my money would be on Suffolk. And because Suffolk farmers like to keep their farmhouses in the family, they are less inclined to boast about those than they are about their stock or their crops, which they want to turn into money.

More than thirty years ago, while collecting material for a book I was writing on Suffolk, I pulled up outside a magnificent farmhouse that had previously caught my eye by a notice on the gate advertising fruit for sale. After spending an odd pound or two, I commented on the house reminding me of a well-known Suffolk manor-house in a neighbouring parish. 'Same builder,' said the farmer without looking up. When I continued to show interest, he told that there were five farmhouses in the district all built by the same family of master builders and carpenters who had been building farmhouses in Suffolk for generations. One had been bought shortly after the end of the Second World War by a wealthy man who consulted a London architect about restoring it. He was warned by the architect not to touch any part of it until he had been able to survey the whole of the property. The new owner then confessed that he had already spoken to a local builder. Builder and architect met, with the result that the new owner was advised to put himself completely in the hands of the local man, with the final remark: 'His craft is bred in him. He couldn't go wrong if he tried.'

Though W.G. Hoskins claims that poets make the best topographers, for Suffolk the best interpreter is Constable. With him in paint, as with Hardy in words, and the country builder just mentioned, understanding was inbred. And neither Constable nor Hardy expected the attitude of the fashionable, sophisticated world to be other than it was. In sending the most famous of his paintings, *The Hay Wain*, to be exhibited in Paris in 1821 – when he was forty-five and at the height of his powers – he wrote: 'Think of the lovely valleys and peaceful farmhouses of Suffolk forming part of an exhibition to amuse the gay Parisians.' Wander down any Suffolk lane today and you will see a farmstead that might have come straight out of one of Constables's landscapes. Suffolk farmhouses are still farmers' houses, and East Anglians are proud that they should be so.

5. Essex Farmhouses

Weatherboarding on Essex farmhouse

One of the attractions of Essex as a Home County is that its countryside starts within ten miles of some of the most densely populated boroughs of Greater London. The best approach to this is along the old coach road into East Anglia which runs between the ancient forests of Hainault and Epping to reach Chigwell, where Dickens stayed at the King's Head – the 'Maypole' of *Barnaby Rudge* – and wrote to his friend Forster, 'Chigwell, my dear fellow, is the greatest place in the world … such an out-of-the-way rural place.' From Chigwell the road continues close to the watermeadows of the River Roding to Abridge and Passingford Bridge, with its timber-framed, weatherboarded watermill, which is as quintessentially Essex in character as any of the churches or farmhouses. From either Abridge or Passingford Bridge it is possible for the motorist to spend an entire day driving through

79

parishes in which Tudor farmhouses are as much part of the rural scene as winding lanes with wide grass verges, wayside inns and windmills.

The Royal Commission on Historical Monuments found medieval carpentry at the core of Essex farmhouses so widespread that it amounted to 'a remarkable commentary on the social and economic history' of the county, and as such were 'of much greater importance than the ecclesiastical' buildings. Most of them were of the timbered hall type, with catslide roofs at the rear descending to within a few feet of the ground, a not inconsiderable number dating from thirteenth or fourteenth century. It was a judgement that must have astonished many who read it in 1923, when few people thought much of either the domestic or any other architecture in Essex apart from such national monuments as Waltham Abbey and Audley End mansion in the west, and Colchester and Hedingham castles in the east.

The distinctive character of the county's domestic buildings, which so surprised the Commissioners, was initially derived from manorial influence being so much stronger than monastic throughout the Middle Ages, when Essex had neither a great abbey with wealth comparable with that of St Edmundsbury in Suffolk nor religious foundations with influence as far reaching as that of the cathedral Priory of Canterbury in Kent. What it did have was an abundance of good oak, which in the hands of skilled carpenters had guaranteed sound construction. The strength of medieval jointing in Essex was demonstrated to me personally during the Second World War while I was a guest in a fifteenth-century timber-framed Essex farmhouse during an air raid. Bombs fell all round it. The building rocked and groaned but suffered no serious damage, and when the raid was over, my host gleefully commented on the shrewdness of his Essex ancestors in building timber-framed houses for siting on Essex clay.

In fact, they had no choice. Essex never had any good building stone, and it had fewer well-drained sites than its neighbours. It is a county of low rainfall but with many springs on the glacial deposits that form low hills inland, and mounds on the water-logged coastal marshes similar to those found in the Fens. In such a terrain the farmhouses were built on dry sites near springs that had never been

Mary Arden's House, Wilmcote, Warwickshire: showing light-coloured timbers and stone slates. It is claimed to be the home of William Shakespeare's mother and makes for an interesting comparison with the somewhat sombre appearance of its thatched near-contemporary in Shottery

Anne Hathaway's Cottage, Shottery, Warwickshire: this part 15th-, part 16th-century cottage is the former home of William Shakespeare's wife

Manor Farm, Wootton Wawen, Warwickshire: a timber-framed and white-painted brick farmhouse of which the distinctive feature is its large door hood decorated with flowers and fruit

Yew Tree Farm, Wootton Wawen, Warwickshire: representative of the many fine red brick farmhouses in the county which sometimes rise to two or more upper storeys

Home Farm, Fen Drayton, Cambridgeshire: the village of Fen Drayton has much to show in the variety of its buildings ranging in period from the present to the 17th century, and in styles from brick to timber-framing

Old Manor Farm, Fen Drayton, Cambridgeshire: thatched, timber-framed and with steep brick gables, this farm has received a Civic Trust award for its conversion into three homes

Church Farm, Boxworth, Cambridgeshire: a double-pile farmhouse of Georgian brick with light yellow pantiles characteristic of East Anglia

Dear's Farm, Elsworth,
Cambridgeshire: thatched with
reed and dating from the early
17th century

The Hall, Fulmodestone, Norfolk: a gracefully proportioned house with a
roof of black pantiles. Depicted in relief on the central pediment is a
shepherd with his dog and two sheep

The Manor, Snettisham, Norfolk: an example of the use of carstone, a dark brown sandstone that has been quarried locally, and the practice of galleting — the painstaking insertion, for their decorative effect, of lines of very small stones along the mortar courses

Croxton Farm, Croxton, Norfolk: parts are thought to date from 1570. The red-pantiled roof, which replaces an earlier thatched one, and the flint facing are characteristic of Norfolk. The use of brick at the corners of a building gives added strength to flint or pebble walls that might otherwise lack stability

The Elms, Walpole, Suffolk: this ex-farmhouse has a brick chimney stack dated 1613, fine pargetting, the cartouche of which is dated 1708, casement windows, and some primitive wall paintings

Street Farm, Earl Soham, Suffolk: built of wattle and daub it has partially-bowed windows which are 300 years old and still retain their original glass panes

Twin Cottages, Withersfield, Suffolk: a feature in Suffolk is for plaster to be colour-washed, traditionally with the red juice of sloes mixed with the black juice of damsons

Moat Hall, Parham, Suffolk: once an abode of the Willoughby family, this 16th-century house is an intriguing combination of timber-framing and early brickwork

known to fail, whose water could be contained in a moat. Moats were dug out for defensive reasons during the Wars of the Roses in many places. In Essex they were primarily for domestic and farm use, and their age can be dated from the original buildings on the site, many of which turn out to have been erected in the fourteenth century.

It was the scarcity of well-drained sites near water that dictated the original choice for a building, and its retention when a larger house was required. So in Essex the core of the original medieval house has been retained intact to a degree probably unmatched in number in any other part of England, although in many it is now concealed behind eighteenth- and nineteenth-century accretions which make its presence unsuspected from a cursory glance at the exterior. The recent work of Cecil Hewett in Essex has resulted in many timber-framed buildings now being reliably attributed to a date a hundred years or more earlier than that given by the Royal Commission. The great barns at Cressing Temple are examples. Until recently the barley barn was dated *c.*1450, the wheat barn *c.*1530. Both have now been redated on jointing evidence, corroborated by Carbon 14 testing, as thirteenth-century. Less scientific but no less convincing evidence of age can be obtained by climbing through manholes in the ceilings of old farmhouses and finding smoke-blackened rafters which prove that they were there when the house was heated from a single open fire on the floor of the hall.

If we compare timber-framed farmhouses in Essex with the Wealden houses of Kent, we see that, whereas those in Kent were built to an ambitious final plan when the timbers were first assembled, those in less prosperous Essex were originally narrow halls of the simplest kind and evolved to their present form as cross-wings were added in the sixteenth and seventeenth centuries. One or both of these may be wider than the hall. Like Essex churches, Essex farmhouses are fascinating medleys, more interesting perhaps to the local historian than to the architect. Most of them remain true to the traditional Essex style of being fully plastered on the outside, although timber-framed. Unfortunately, early in the present century, when Essex came into the London commuter belt, it became fashionable to strip off the plaster and display the timbers. For a few years the urge to do this spread like an epidemic across the county, but it died out when it was realized that the plaster was to keep out the wind. Buildings treated in this way can often be recognized by rust stains on the studs, left by the nails which fixed the laths supporting the plaster.

In the spider's web of lanes north-west of the main road from Passingford Bridge to Ongar, with Greensted's only Saxon surviving timber nave (*c.850*) in England at the heart of them, churches and farmhouses continue in intimate relationship, most of them originally built by estate masons and carpenters. One could hardly imagine greater variety in so small a region. Great Tawney Hall, for example, which is by no means a self-conscious showpiece, is a good case of a small timber-framed farmhouse being built up to manor-house status. Part of the weatherboard cladding on what was formerly an outshut has been retained in the present double-pile plan, in which it was built up to provide first-floor rooms under a separate roof. Both these roofs, with a valley between them, appear to have been renewed in the nineteenth century, when the handsome red-brick front was built, with a parapet to give it height. Nine sash windows and an elegant front door at the head of flight of steps finally conferred an honest dignity to the house, while leaving evidence of its humble ancestry at the rear.

In the four Hundreds of Ongar, Harlow, Dunmow and Chelmsford, with Felsted thrown in for good measure, the 1923 Royal Commission listed more than 120 farmhouses worthy of preservation. It would be impossible to do justice to more than a few representative examples in the space available here, and selection might be invidious. In practically all of them the hall has remained unbroken at the core, either with or without aisles or screen passages. As most of these houses are in parishes that have recently suffered urban infiltration, they are all the more remarkable in having retained so many original features inside. New ownership so often results in conventional period features being retained outside, which are found to be no more than a deceptive facade to what has been done inside.

Fyfield Hall, north of Ongar, is an outstanding example of a medieval timber-framed farmhouse, extended and adapted to new needs instead of being replaced when a larger house was required. It was built in the fourteenth century – possibly early in the century – as a hall-house with two aisles. One of these was probably sacrificed when a ceiling was inserted in the hall. The other was saved in a remarkable manner. At the beginning of the sixteenth century a two-storeyed range was built alongside the hall, parallel with it without being destructively integrated into it. To have such an anticipation of the double-pile plan so early must be very rare indeed.

This plastered, timber-framed range is now the main front of the house and, although much altered, still retains a long moulded bressumer carved with running foliage, supported by brackets carved in sixteenth-century style. The nail-studded door appears to be original. Three gabled wings were added at different dates from the sixteenth to the eighteenth century.

In Lampetts, Dame Anna's Farm and Ponders Lodge Farm, Fyfield had three other important timber-framed farmhouses, and every parish in the surrounding countryside of the Lavers, the Roothings – as Essex people call the Rodings – and the Easters has fine old hall-houses, many of which are all the more interesting for not being showpieces. Three-quarters of a mile north of Beauchamp Roding church is Longbarns, timber-framed, with three gables, sixteenth- and seventeenth-century chimneystacks and original barge-boarding. Colville Hall in White Roding is a fifteenth-century farmhouse with sixteenth- and seventeenth-century additions made while it was the property of the Browne family, who also owned Rookwood Hall, of which only a fragment remains of the house in which Elizabeth I held a Privy Council in 1578. Cammas Hall, the manor-house of the defunct parish of Morrell Roding, which has so long been in the care of John Lukies, one of the county's most respected farmers, worthily completes this fine group of farmhouses in the heart of Essex. The record of the Royal Commission is currently being followed up and reassessed in the volumes of the *Victoria County History of Essex*, of which eight have been published since 1951.

The danger of judging from outside appearances has been emphasized in Essex recently by two scholarly works on farmhouses referring to Whiteheads, Hatfield Broad Oak, as

Farmhouse with typical extensions, Shalford

'demolished'. Much of it has been rebuilt, but the central block is a faithful replacement of the original hall. The wings have been made symmetrical, probably in a rebuilding earlier than that of the original hall. The value of the building for students of periods of rebuilding in relation to local farming prosperity is that much of the work at Whiteheads must have been carried out during the wave of vigorous farmhouse building and rebuilding which started about 1575.

The central chimneystack is interesting in that, like many of the period, it was built to take the smoke from two hearths, one in the hall, the other in the south-east cross wing, and was later adapted to serve fires on the first floor. With so little of the building left unaltered, it is difficult even to hazard a guess as to its date, but the 1560 appearing on the house may be thought earlier than anything seen today.

The enlargement of hall farmhouses in Essex in the last quarter of the sixteenth and first half of the seventeenth century is obvious evidence of prosperity, but such features as the bringing into symmetry of cross wings seems to suggest a desire among yeomen for recognition of status, which might be compared with the building by the gentry of long galleries, most of which have been demolished. But there is one feature prominent in Essex dating from this period that we can hardly interpret as anything but a bid for recognition of status, namely ornate chimneystacks.

At the same time we must recognize that chimneystacks fulfilled many utilitarian as well as decorative purposes in addition to the carrying away of smoke. They were often positioned to stablize the structure. In the larger hall-houses with cross wings, a massive axial chimneybreast could be built in the middle of the hall. In those with only one cross wing, it was usual to build it against the wall separating the hall from the wing so substantially that the entire house hung on it. A third custom was to build chimneystacks at both ends, usually at different dates before the Georgian plan was introduced. A fourth was to build a wing at the rear of the hall which could take both a chimneystack and a staircase. These staircase wings are features of sixteenth- and seventeenth-century farmhouses in the north-west of the county, which continued in favour in the eighteenth where it was not feasible to build in any other part of the building without either loss of space or a risk of weakening the structure.

The best part of the county for seeing status chimneystacks is the fertile heart of Essex ploughland round Chelmsford. A house within a hundred yards of Boreham church has two fifteenth-century diagonal shafts, corbelled and crow-stepped at the top. Most Essex chimneystacks are sixteenth-century and octagonal. Some have two shafts, Priors at Broomfield has four, Woodend Farm at Beauchamp Roding six. Greenfields at Felsted has a chimneystack with three panels, one decorated with a circle, one with a diamond, and one with a *fleur-de-lis*, the heraldic lily borne in the royal arms of France. Dukes at Roxwell is unique in that each of the three original chimneystacks has three octagonal shafts on a rectangular base, with a deep band at the top diapered with quatrefoils. The most elaborate chimneyshafts on a building of moderate size are on the beautifully restored house now called the Guildhall, twenty yards east of the church at Great Waltham, which has seven tall shafts with moulded capitals and bases, each with a decorative plaster panel.

The main division in Essex for the purpose of exploring farmhouse styles is between chalk and clay. Most of the farmhouses already described are on the heavy clay of mid-Essex, where descriptive place-names with endings like 'field' and 'stead' indicate clearance of the forest, which at one time covered the greater part of the county, much later than where names end in 'ing', 'ham' and 'ton', as they do along the river banks first settled by Saxon invaders. The chalk is mainly in the undulating downland of north-west Essex, where the Audley End estate gives unity to farmhouse styles. The Manor House, Great Chesterford, for example, was built *c.*1500 on the usual rectangular plan but instead of being given cross wings had a wing added at the rear to make it L-shaped, which is another style characteristic of north Essex. St Aylotts, on a moated site two miles north-east of Saffron Walden, is of approximately the same date and is one of many buildings in north Essex and Suffolk which illustrate the skill of carpenters working in the eastern counties at the time. The carved angle-brackets, the moulded bressumers of the upper storey, the small bay window in the pantry and the internal doorways and fireplaces are all of a very high order. Two projecting chimneystacks are stepped above the eaves, with shafts of different design and diagonal pilasters. Between them are joint marks indicating the position of a former oval window in the hall. Near the south end of the north-east elevation is a projecting stair-turret.

From this north-west corner of Essex, the Cambridgeshire border should be crossed out of Great Chesterford into Ickleton, a village that is an object lesson for local historians puzzled by lack of unity in architectural styles. Ickleton, incidentally, has one of the finest churches in East Anglia and one of the least known. It has also an exceptionally interesting group of small manor-houses which were formerly farmhouses, only one of which (Abbey Farm, 1692) is built entirely of Cambridgeshire clunch, with walls three feet thick. The clue to the diversity of styles is again to be found in the names. The Caldrees derives its name from the abbey of Calders in Cumberland, to which it once belonged, Durhams from Dereham in Norfolk, Fullen House from being near the old fulling-mill, Frogge Hall from its waterside site, and Mowbrats from having been the property of the Mowbray dukes of Norfolk before it was acquired by Clare College, Cambridge. Apart from Abbey Farm, all are timber-framed but they have been restored and altered in different ways, which is no doubt due to estate carpenters from widely separated parts of England having worked on them. This variety of styles is all the more striking by being in such sharp contrast to the unity that distinguishes farmhouses on the wide-ranging Audley End estate. Students confronted with such divergences in neighbouring parishes will often find it useful to look up the descents of the manors, which are recorded in the relevant volume of the county's *Victoria County History*.

The walls in nearly all the old farmhouses in north-west Essex have retained their plaster. This is found particularly effective for houses in which chalk is the basis of the plaster used for infilling the spaces between the studs. This was done by inserting wattle panels, which were sprung into the framework and well packed with plaster. When renewals were required because the old plaster was crumbling, one of two forms of cladding might be used: brick-nogging or weatherboarding, with weatherboarding normally favoured in Essex. This explains why most of the farmhouses in the region, and in Essex generally, will be found to have sections weatherboarded. It can be seen especially at Felsted, one of the best parishes in which to see old farmhouses maintained in true Essex style. Among the most characteristic are Chaffix, Oxneys, Sparlings and Bridgehouse farmhouses – all fifteenth-century or only slightly later. Sparlings and Bridgehouse, Thistley Green, have halls still open to the roof.

While in the Felsted neighbourhood, Terling might be visited for its seventeenth-century group of farmhouses as a sequel to the fifteenth-century farmhouses to the north. The chimneystack at the Manor House, Terling, is of that date. So is the central stack at Sparrows Farm, which has vertical flutings on a square base. In the final stages of development in Essex, as in Suffolk, a lath-and-plaster building, with laths nailed onto the studs or battens between them and plastered both externally and internally, made a very effective structure. Straw was sometimes packed between the two claddings, and when the wattle frame was ready for fixing, both sides were well covered with daub, which consisted in the clay belt of the county of wet clay or mud firmly consolidated with chopped straw, cowhair and dung. A smooth coating of lime plaster was the final stage. One such house on a busy high street, is certainly both warm and remarkably sound-proof, although its sash windows are not double-glazed.

The use of weatherboarding in Essex and Kent becomes so familiar that one tends to forget how restricted its range of use was in England, despite the 'Colonial style', as it is called in New England, having been our most nostalgic export in domestic architecture to America and parts of Canada. It is comparatively rare in Hertfordshire and can nowhere be considered vernacular in Buckinghamshire. The explanation may be that brickmaking developed early in the region for domestic buildings as well as for monastic buildings and castles, so although timber-framed farmhouses are distinctive in Essex, brick buildings are historically of prime importance.

There are ten farmhouses in Essex called Brick House or Brickhouse Farm. Most of them are eighteenth-century, but several are sixteenth-century. The most imposing brickwork in an old farmhouse is at Bradfield Hall, overlooking the Stour Estuary in the north-east corner of the county. It has a superb crow-stepped brick south front, with moulded copings and crocketed pinnacles set diagonally which have every appearance of being early sixteenth-century. The brickwork of the walls is diapered, and at the south-west angle there is a semi-octagonal stair turret of *c*.1600.

Stanway, on the old London road, has more than one old farmhouse encased in eighteenth-century brick, which is, in fact, timber-framed. Catchbells is one that may catch the eye because it is close to the road. Beacon End Farm, Stanway, now a charming two-storeyed farmhouse with cross wings under a hipped roof, apparently eighteenth-century, retains joists and tie beams of the original fourteenth-century hall-house, into which a chimneybreast was built *c*.1500 and a ceiling inserted in the sixteenth century.

The outstanding example of a medieval house deceptively encased in brick is in the north-west of the county in the large, scattered parish of Wimbish. It takes its name from Sir John Tiptoft, who lived in it from 1348 to 1367, and has a complete fourteenth-century aisled hall dating from Sir John's time, open to the roof and showing how closely secular buildings of the period resembled ecclesiastical in their timbering. The piers support traceried curved braces carved with the motif of a pointed trefoil. The octagonal king post on the tie beam is like those in small country churches, but the most arresting feature is the introduction of hammerbeams into a domestic building soon after the middle of the fourteenth century. A two-centred arch with decorated spandrels, which clearly was not the only one, indicates that there were doors leading into either a buttery for the storage of ale or a pantry for bread. Whichever was the one from which the existing arch is preserved, the other may be presumed to have been there. Thunderley Hall and Abbots Manor are two other medieval houses in the same parish. But the most interesting historically is Broadoaks, two miles south-south-east of the church at Wimbish, the old home of the great Roman Catholic family of Wiseman.

Broadoaks, or Braddocks as it is commonly known, is a moated brick house of *c.*1560 but unhappily incomplete. What survives is only one arm of the original E-shaped building; but such features as the six-light window on the ground floor, the six-light window with two transoms on the first floor, and the four-light window in one of the gables gives some idea of the elegance of the rooms in the house when the Wisemans lived there. There is a fine classical stone fireplace in the main room, which was on the first floor, and the surviving chimneystacks, with tall octagonal shafts, bear testimony to the period of Catholic persecution, when priests were concealed in holes in such chimneybreasts and brought out of hiding to say Mass to the faithful.

All these houses would be known to William Harrison, the Elizabethan chronicler, who wrote his *Description of England* in the reign of the first Elizabeth ('this foule frizled Treatise of mine', he called it) in the study of his parsonage at Radwinter in the next parish, where he farmed his glebe like any other country parson and watched his wife and her maidservants brew the household beer. The buildings that have been described can be read like books today by anyone with knowledge of what each feature signifies, but we still need William Harrison's account, supplemented by those of other parson diarists, to furnish these farmhouses for us. We need also the wills that have been transcribed so painstakingly for us by Dr. Emmison. They complete the houses that Elizabeth would have seen as she moved from one Great House to another in her Progresses through the eastern counties.

From William Harrison we learn that the greatest advance in moveable furniture in his time had been the introduction of permanent bedsteads, but those of even yeomen farmers were still trestles. In wills we find an abundance of evidence that the kind of farmhouses we have been discussing would have large chests packed with bed linen. Sheets are specified as being of hemp, buckram, Holland, flax or linen; blankets are particularized, and 'coverlids' appear, worked with floral designs. All these may be presumed to have been in use in Tiptofts, Broadoaks, St Aylotts and the halls of both Great and Little Chesterford, which would be in Harrison's mind when he wrote of farmers having beds 'furnished with silk hangings, and their tables with fine naperie'.

Walls would be decorated with samplers and 'posies', which were moral sentiments condensed into rhymed couplets for inscribing on the walls of bed-chambers, as texts were inscribed on the walls of churches. They were the prototypes of the pious sentiments framed in floral-design borders, of which violets and pansies were the favourites, that hung on the bedroom walls of most farmhouses in Victorian times. Tusser, the Essex farmer who wrote rhymed manuals of instruction for farmers (although a failure himself), composed posies for his friends. His 'posy for a parlour' may be taken as typical:

Hast thou a friend as heart may wish it will?
Then use him so to have his friendship still.

Both Tusser and Harrison wrote in what appeared to them to be a period of great promise for Essex agriculture, but despite all the advantages the county had in climate and soil, the magnetism of London became too great for enterprising young farmers to resist. It offered greater rewards in employment with less labour. So this county with its unique heritage of Tudor farmhouses drifted into a period of agricultural stagnation. The tide was reversed when the expansion of London into Essex provided new markets for dairy produce, and enterprising Scottish and Somerset farming families came in to take advantage of it, immeasurably enriching the county's social and economic life. I remember meeting a middle-aged man on the road from Epping to Chelmsford forty years ago. He had returned to see his home county again after prospering in Australia. I made the conventional remark that it was sometimes inviting disillusionment to return to scenes that memory had romanticized. This was not his experience, he said. The present prosperity of the county had astonished him.

As we drove between fields he had known well when he lived in Essex, he recalled the days when farms were badly equipped and wages little above starvation level. The only breaks for labourers came on rainy days. There were no breaks for the women, who on washing days stood for weary hours at the wash-tub or copper boiler, dollying, scrubbing and wringing clothes. Few farmhouses had piped water, although the larger ones might have a hand-worked pump in the middle of the kitchen floor, like one I remember at Fyfield. But Essex folk were cheerful by nature, and the men who worked in the fields derived satisfaction from ploughing a straight furrow, hoeing in a line of fellow-workers between rows of springing corn, or pulling and clamping roots for winter feed. As late as 1926, a special meeting of the local committee had to be called when it was learned that the coveted and valuable challenge cup in the Ploughing Match had been won by a man who slept in the stable with his horses, so provision would have to be made for its safe-keeping.

The climax of the year was, of course, the harvest, with morning breaks for 'beevers' of barley beer and bread and cheese made piquant with onions. An earthenware harvest jug was passed round, firmly stoppered but with a spout from which each harvester in turn might take a swig.

I heard how the last sheaves were raced for and made into corn dollies, and how at the end the 'lord of the harvest' would stand with his team in the middle of the field awaiting the arrival of the farmer, whose appearance would be greeted with a chorus of voices calling for largesse – the harvest bounty. Finally there was the harvest supper, with roast beef, hot custard or apple pie and spiced ale. 'And', he concluded, 'Gad! they had earned it!'

6. The Kent and Sussex Weald House

Old Bell Farm, a Wealden house

The timber-framed hall houses of the Kent and Sussex Weald are in a class of their own. The Weald was the 'Black Country' of the Middle Ages, deriving wealth from iron-smelting for hundreds of years before the fertility of the clearings made it 'the Garden of England'. The felling of oaks to feed the furnaces was a slow and sporadic process, which meant that the region was settled in isolated steads. It has therefore no history of compact villages, and little evidence of community strip cultivation, villeinage or tenancy by service. With no overlords to confiscate timber for their own use, the iron-masters were an idependent race, and with abundant straight-stemmed oaks they were able to build the stalwart, well-proportioned houses which set the pattern for the farmhouses

93

which succeeded them and which represent so enduringly the steadfast qualities of the English yeoman. We now tend to forget that such houses as Kipling's Bateman's at Burwash were built by ironmasters. Despite this, the proprietory use of the name 'yeoman's house', as an alternative to Wealden house, for the Kentish style of hall house is not as presumptuous as it may sound. There were far more independent freeholders in Kent in the fifteenth-century than anywhere else in England.

The special character of the Kent and Sussex Weald house is in the way practically all its features conform to a basic pattern. At the core is the hall, which gives the type generally its name and common denominator. This is larger in the Wealden plan than in those of other well-wooded areas. So when in Kent and Sussex the house was extended laterally with double-storeyed wings, these were constructed not under separate roofs, as in Essex, but in stout timber frames which projected a mere foot forward from the hall line, enabling the entire structure to be accommodated under a single roof. The external braces supporting this massive roof – which other counties got later – were in use in Kent by the end of the fourteenth century. We see them at Stone Hall Farm, near Chiddingly, and in Sussex on the Clergy House at Alfriston. But despite the finality of the Kent and Sussex Weald house, we find Continental influences apparent, as in the hall houses all the way down the eastern side of England. This was probably because many of them were copied directly from Flemish pattern-books.

By the end of the sixteenth century the typical yeoman's house in Kent had six or seven rooms. Some had nine or more, yet the principal bedroom was still on the ground floor. All had hall, buttery and pantry, but only the largest had rooms referred to as kitchens, which means that in most of them the food was still cooked and eaten in the hall. When dating is in doubt, it is useful to remember that timbers in the earliest were marked at the joints with Roman numerals incised in them, and that genuine adze smoothing can often be recognized by bearing in mind that an adze had the blade twisted round like that of a hoe.

The timber used for the frame was invariably oak, which was normally less wind-bent in Kent than in the West Midlands, so crucks can never have been as common there as they were in counties with less depth of soil. There were certainly enough straight trunks at hand for all the posts required to support the massive roof timbers, which are bolder and plainer than even those in Suffolk, and much less demonstrative than those decorated with the ornate carpentry found along the Welsh Marches. Heavy posts eight or nine inches square were fixed upright seven or eight feet apart into a foundation wall, with heavier posts at the angles. These angle posts were formed of the butts of trees placed root upwards with the top part curving diagonally outwards to carry the angle posts of the upper storey, as seen at Pattenden and Swaylands, near Penshurst in Kent.

A perfect model of the typical Wealden house has been reconstructed at the Weald and Downland Air Museum at Singleton, near Chichester. Such houses are superbly suited to be the homes of men like the old yeoman who figures in the lines: 'Here comes old Woodcock, the yeoman of Kent, that's half Farmer and half Gentleman; his horses go to the plow all Week, and are put into the coach o' Sunday.'* That 'old Woodcock' was representative of his class is confirmed by Lambarde, the Kent historian, who wrote in *The Perambulation of Kent* (1574): 'A man may find sundry yeomen (although otherwise for wealth comparable with many of the gentle sort) that will not yet for all that, change their condition nor desire to be apparelled with the titles of Gentry.'

The highest concentration of the finest Kentish Wealden farmhouses is in the strip of country south-west of the North Downs and east of a line drawn from Sevenoaks in Kent to Battle in Sussex. In most of them the entire structure is stablized by an enormous central chimneystack carrying the flues of four chimneys, wide enough at the base to provide back-to-back space for blazing log hearths in both the Hall and the living kitchen, along with ingle-nooks in the one and in the other space for cauldrons, spits and ovens to meet every need.

These great chimneystacks frequently boast octagonal, hexagonal or spiral chimneys that might seem out of keeping with the basic simplicity of the timberwork but are invariably well designed and

---

*Tunbridge Walks, or *The Yeoman of Kent*, Act 1, sc.i

95

dignified. The pots at the head of them are, of course, later and of designs that are not always either artistically inspired or scientifically devised. Indoors all is well! The fireplace is almost invariably spanned by a chamfered oak beam, which is another indication of the yeoman's innate feeling for timber. The brickwork at the back of open hearth is usually protected by a cast-iron fireback, made by casting molten iron into a prepared sand mould sculped to produce a Tudor rose or the owner's initials, often in a well-designed monogram accompanied by the date in clear figures. Some were obviously provided by the landowner who built the farmhouse, in the way Victorian landowners had their family badge on their properties. Probably the commonest family badge on old Sussex firebacks is the buckle of the Pelham family.

Modern chimney backs can be recognized by being so much lighter in weight and having merely conventional designs. At one time many of these mass-produced firebacks came from either the Low Countries or France. They must have been valued more as fireside furniture than for any protection they gave. Early this century, farmhouse fires that got out of hand and set the building ablaze were attributed to beams running into the chimneystack becoming overheated. Apparently, most of them were caused by soot accumulating in cavities in the chimney walls catching fire, and there is considerable evidence that not sufficient care was taken to build the flues with sides free from projecting ledges.

The basket-shaped grates that have recently come back into fashion for log fires – although more appropriate for coal, since they allow the valuable ash from wood to fall through – came into use along with Dutch ovens in the second half of the seventeenth-century.

It is good to see so many fireplaces in Wealden farmhouses being furnished again with ironware from local forges. The old fireplaces were more than three feet deep and up to ten feet wide, so must be visualized as part of the chimneystack. They are always fully lined with brick and may have a brick oven at the side. If the chimneystacks are at the end of the building, as many are, the upper stages are reduced progressively by a series of 'corbie' steps of the kind commonest in East Anglia. In both regions they show Dutch or Flemish influence. But despite this tapering by stages, the flues of early chimneys do tend to be exceptionally wide in Kent and Sussex farmhouses, with the result that south of the Thames they are usually dominant features to a greater degree than they are in Essex and East Anglia. This obviously indicates that little thought was given to the fuel they would consume.

The impression of massed strength is completed with the roofs, which are hipped and roofed with heavy stone slabs, usually from the famous Horsham quarries or others which assumed their name. Kent has, in fact, a rich variety of local stone. The fixing of these stone slabs could be a tricky business. In Kent and Sussex they are usually hung on wooden pegs. As in Essex, wooden gutters and pipes were formerly used to carry off the water. These were usually of elm and were skilfully bored to get good joints at each end of a length of piping. When used for field drainage they were extremely effective and continue to be dug up from time to time in Essex – and no doubt in Kent – to this day.

The oldest roofs in Wealden houses did not have dormers set back from the eaves. From the sixteenth century, gables were built up from the timber frontage in the South-East as they were from stone frontages in the Cotswolds. A favourite device in Kent and Sussex was to build up the gables from the square head of a mullioned window. This is seen in the exceptionally fine yeoman's house, Synyards, in the hop gardens three miles south-west of Maidstone, a house of the same type as the one rebuilt at the Weald and Downland Museum – a forthright house with an overhanging upper storey and a steeply pitched continuous hipped roof. Otham has three other magnificent yeomen's houses of the fourteenth to fifteenth centuries: Gore Court (fifteenth-seventeenth), Wardes (fourteenth-sixteenth) and Stoneacre (fifteenth-sixteenth), reached up a steep lane and of special interest because, although modifications were made in the sixteenth century, it is substantially a magnificent yeoman's house, with hall and solar of *c.*1480. Stoneacre was given to the National Trust by Aymer Vallance, the distinguished Kent ecclesiologist, whose home it was.

The yeomen of Kent probably pioneered in England the inserting of a floor at one end of their large halls to support a private chamber, which would be followed quickly by one at the other end, leaving the spacious hall unaltered between them.

97

Unfortunately the specific use of such words as 'chamber' and 'parlour' in local records is not a safe clue to either date or use. The word 'chamber', which was introduced into England in the Middle Ages, continued to be used for bedrooms in Kent until the seventeenth century.

The most we can say about the use of 'chamber' and 'parlour' in England generally is that they appear to have divided the country between them. South of a line from King's Lynn to Shrewsbury the rooms that are called parlours to the north are called chambers. At the same time, it may be noted that the word 'chamber' was always distinctively a first-floor room, while parlours were on the ground floor and were specially associated with stone rather than timber-framed houses. The word 'parlour' – the name of the room in which monks were allowed to indulge in conversation – was adopted by the gentry of Yorkshire, a strongly ecclesiastical county, for the room previously called the bower immediately after the Dissolution. What may be deduced from the early and continuous use of the word 'chamber' for 'bedroom' in the south-east is that bedrooms were transferred upstairs in that part of the country long before they were in the north, where beds continued to be in living-room recesses in remote dales until within living memory. They may survive in upper Teesdale to this day.

Some of the best farm- and manor-houses in the Weald had been built with upper floors jettied out from end to end from the close of the fifteenth century. The idea for this may have come from the guilds, which were already strong in small towns in Kent long before they were in East Anglia. Evidence for this may be found in parish churches. Where the aisles are much wider than would be required for processional purposes, they were usually built in this way to accommodate guild altars. Where the aisle width in town churches is not more than was normal in the fifteenth century, it is often useful to enquire into the original use of any fifteenth-century secular building that has a continuous overhanging storey. It may well turn out to have been a guildhall.

In the majority of fifteenth- and sixteenth-century hall houses in Kent, as elsewhere, the upper floor will be found to have been inserted in the seventeenth century, when large halls might be divided into two living-rooms with a cross passage between them.

In others, where there was ample space in other parts of the building for introducing new rooms, the great hall was still regarded as so fundamental a part of the family home that to cut it up would be sacrilege. It *was* the home, so money was spent in providing it with a magnificent Jacobean staircase leading to a gallery providing communication between the wings.

A good part of the county for finding early examples of yeoman-type farmhouses built without wings under a single roof is around Charing. One of these is fifteenth-century Link Farm at Egerton, four miles south-west of Charing. There the entrance is at the lower end of the hall, which must have been divided early into two storeys. Although one of the two projecting upper rooms is larger than the other, this does not, as it probably would in Essex, indicate that it was added when the farmer could afford a better wing. It merely meant that it was designed to have the best room in it. In short, the timber-framed houses in Kent were not built in instalments to the extent they were in poorer parts of England. They were built as a rule by men who already had the money to pay for all they wanted when the foundations were laid.

Different sizes of rooms appear to have been just as intentionally planned at Combe Farm, Chiddingfold, where the gables of the wings are of different sizes. The explanation there would be that the rooms in the larger wing were for family use, the smaller ones for offices. We see this kind of intentional irregularity at Milford in Surrey. Midway between Charing and Maidstone is Old Bell Farm, an outstandingly fine example of a Kentish yeoman's house of the late fifteenth century, with three doorways in the twenty-five-foot-long rear wall of the hall, one leading into the pantry, a second into the buttery, and a third to the staircase leading to the chamber above. Houses of this size dating from the fifteenth century are rare anywhere.

The farmhouses of the Sussex Weald are similar to those of Kent, but Sussex foundries were fed with timber so recklessly that in 1664 John Evelyn advocated moving all the 'devouring iron mills' to New England, 'for they will ruin Old England'. It would be better, he argued, 'to purchase all our iron out of America than thus to exhaust our woods at home'. Oak had been so abundant in the Weald that it was called 'the Sussex weed'.

Eventually the prudent yeomen of the Weald realized how destructive of every local interest this reckless felling of timber would be if it continued much longer. So what was called half-timbering was introduced, with thinner timbers wider apart built into the structure in square or oblong panels to be filled with wattle-and-daub in the East Anglian manner. But in Kent, as early as Elizabeth I's reign, tiles were being used for wall cladding as well as roofing, and they became the most popular outer coat for half-timbered buildings as well as for those built up to first-floor level in brick. Leases and deeds of sales negotiated by Kentish yeomen show how widely dispersed these local brick- and tile-works were. The Kent surname Hillier, which means tiler, is further evidence. Other indentures of Elizabeth's reign now show that local lime- and brickworks were numerous in all the south-eastern counties in the seventeenth century, although there is little evidence of Kent and Sussex farmhouses being plastered and pargeted in the way Essex and Suffolk farmhouses were.

In the later years of the seventeenth century weatherboarding came into competition with hanging tiles for wall cladding. Every rural parish in the South-East today has fine examples of either the one or the other, and most villages in Kent have both. While the trade in these flourished, considerable ingenuity was exercised in varying designs, culminating late in the eighteenth century at Lewes in a mathematically shaped tile designed to lie flat on the building, giving the walls a brick-like appearance while evading the brick taxes. Early in the nineteenth century decoratively shaped tiles were developed in Kent and Sussex when moulding came into use.

In both tiling and boarding the early work was better than the later. Old tiles were thicker and more unevenly burnt, giving them an irregularity of texture and colour which adds immeasurably to their appearance by softening the contours and providing channels and plains to enhance the play of light across them. The colours with which they become dappled by time and weather range from tea-stain browns to orange, terra-cotta and even vermilion, although away from the Weald they are usually nothing more than a cheerful reddish brown. The ridge tiles on old Wealden houses are plain and semi-circular, those of the roof rectangular, drawing their appeal from gently curved surfaces producing subtle

100

gradations of light and shade. The wall tiles were bedded in mortar. Most of those seen today were hung on timber-framed buildings with jettied upper floors, which were showing signs of decay in the eighteenth century. They were strengthened from the ground to first-floor level with brick walls built in front of the timber-frame or plaster.

The earliest weatherboarding was of oak or elm, with wedge-shaped boards about six inches wide laid horizontally and pegged to the timbers so as to overlap one another. When finished, they were either tarred or painted white. Now the houses are all painted white, and only the outhouses may be black, except on exposed coastal sites. That many more were tarred originally is shown in the frequent occurrence of the name 'Black Cottage' in old deeds. Now imported deal is used, which is already being superseded by plastic.

Some of the best weatherboarding in England is to be seen in several large houses at Tenterden, many of which would formerly be farmhouses, and in the town grouping of Cranbrook as well as throughout the Smarden and Charing districts. Charing itself is a showpiece, and Smarden has a street of great interest to the architectural historian because it reflects every aspect of what is most typical of this type of work in this county of beautiful villages.

Hanging tiles are fairly common in old cottages in Hampshire and Berkshire but are extremely rare elsewhere, despite their obvious value in forming a simple and effective form of waterproofing. They were seldom used anywhere to cover the whole of the walling, and one of their most attractive features is the way they were laid to curve out at the base in order to overlap the brick and throw the water clear of the wall, as thatch had done at the eaves before it was superseded by tiled roofs. In old farmhouses the encasing of the whole of the ground floor in brick means that the entire building was brought into harmony with the earlier brick chimneystacks, for which the South-East is unsurpassed.

When iron-smelting moved to the Midlands, the farmers of Kent began to concentrate more on taking advantage of the expanding market for dairy and orchard produce in London. They did this so successfully that in the seventeenth century what had been 'the

Black Country' of the Middle Ages became 'the Garden of England'. There is a tradition that there was little fruit-growing in England before the reign of Henry VIII. The number of places with 'apple' incorporated in their name shows this to be untrue, but apple orchards were universal in England in Elizabeth I's reign, and trees growing pears, cherries and plums were common. It was the marketing of fruit that was rare. This was simply because England was still rural, and every cottage had its own fruit trees. With the expansion of London in the seventeenth century, orchards were planted throughout the Home Counties for the commercial production of fruit, with Kent in the lead. Most of the cherries being 'cried' on the streets – 'Cherry ripe, ripe I cry' – would have come from Kent or Surrey. In 1637 John Shermenden, a Surrey yeoman, mentioned apples, pears, strawberries, raspberries, gooseberries, cherries, damsons, apricots, peaches and quinces in a statement on tithes he owed the vicar.

The farm buildings associated with this new agriculture were oast houses, delightfully built in local vernacular style. It was appropriate that it should be so, since 'oast' means 'kiln', and Kent had lime kilns in the fourteenth century. They also integrate into the historical scene because they belong to the same tradition of mechanical ingenuity as windmills. Hops were introduced into Kent north of the Downs in 1525, but drum-shaped oast houses, capped with a pivoted timber cowl with a flyboard controlled by the wind in the way weathervanes are, were not invented until the 1830s, so were a nineteenth-century innovation. They were followed in the present century by square oasts designed to allow the hops to circulate in horsehair cloth mounted on rollers, but these were short-lived. Hops are now machine-picked and dried by electric fans, roof louvres, and oil-fired heating.

Like windmills in Essex, peles in Northumberland and other relics of the Past, the old oast houses are now either country cottages or annexes to country houses. But it is a very recent Past. Old people in London's East End still look back nostalgically to the time when the harvesting of hops was the great summer event in the Cockney year, with whole families travelling down the Old Kent Road on donkey shays and costermongers' carts to the same hop gardens year after year. The copses from which the hop poles

102

Oasthouses, cooling area between two kilns

were cut are still there, but the posts are now connected with galvanized wire by coir yarn strings.

Among the orchards and hop gardens we may still find splendid Elizabethan farmhouses. One stands opposite the church at Borden, south of Sittingbourne, and Borden Hall to the north of the church is a well-restored Tudor building with a recovered solar fireplace and fine old tithe barn. South of Borden is Bredgar, with Bexon Manor, a fine yeoman's house of the fifteenth to seventeenth centuries, and Milsted, still only three miles from Sittingbourne, retains its old Manor House and Manor Farm. Another group of typically Kentish farmhouses can be visited from Ashford, south of the North Downs.

So farming in Kent still means fruit-growing and market gardening in the north of the county, with spacious farmhouses continuing to add a benevolent sense of well-being to the scene, despite its proximity to London. That so many of these houses are

103

no longer occupied by yeomen need not worry anyone so long as they are cared for and maintained by families with real feeling for what they are and what they represent in an England that is vanishing in all too many parts of the country at an alarmingly accelerating speed.

7. Cotswold Gothic

Dovecot at Bibury, Cotswold

Cotswold stone is much more than part of the belt of limestone which runs transversely across England from Dorset to Yorkshire, producing stone of fine quality along its entire course. Its unique attraction is the way it tones down from a reddish yellow on exposure, through the colour of Gloucester cheese to a soft butter or honey colour, grained with silvery particles that reflect the light to produce a sparkle which no other limestone possesses. The best has the advantage of hardening to a consistency which allows it to be cut without crumbling.

Building with stone has thousands of years behind it in the Cotswolds. The long barrows of Notgrove in the north and Nymphsfield near Uley in the south were built up in drystone walling before being covered with earth. Their slat-thin walls may be as much as four thousand years old. Roman masons taught the natives how to erect buildings for the living as well as the dead, but it was not until the Middle Ages that the distinctive style we call Cotswold Gothic evolved from a combination of lay and monastic skills: the monastic from the work done by the West Midlands schools of craftsmen who produced the great abbeys, the cathedrals and finally the fifteenth-century wool churches of the region, the lay from work done for the Berkeleys of Berkeley Castle, who in the fourteenth century set standards for domestic architecture which filtered through to such minor features as the dovecotes still associated with so many Cotswold manor-houses, and even to the staddle-stones on which small granaries were raised above the wet earth and out of reach of vermin.

The prudence of the farming organized by the monks is shown in the fact that large-scale medieval provision for the storage of grain and other farm produce is found only where monastic granges stood. Every building in the Cotswolds, from the smallest shed to the largest barn, was built in the same style, and well-preserved medieval barns are particularly valuable as records of Cotswold vernacular. Their original purpose was for the storing and winnowing of corn, but later they were even more important for the storing of fleeces claimed as tithe by the landowning abbots and priors after annual sheep-shearings. That is why, although they were not originally built as tithe-barns, it is reasonable to give them that name.

The dovecotes, which are now preserved as amenity features, are really pigeon-houses. The earliest were built when pigeons became an essential source of fresh food in the second half of the thirteenth century. These were cylindrical, with vaulted or domed roofs, the central part open to the sky so that the pigeons could fly out and in again to their nesting holes. Early in their development a massive post was set up in the centre of the dovecote floor from which it could be pivoted, with the upper end fixed into a cross-beam near the roof. From this post projected spokes which were reached from the floor by ladders. The whole mechanism of this egg-collecting contraption was so constructed that it could be revolved by pressing one hand against the wall, the other against a spoke, in order to gain access to all the nesting holes in turn.

The walls of these cylindrical dovecotes were at least three feet thick. They were succeeded by the more typically Cotswold type, which is square, with gables on all four sides and a turret at the top. Their formal architecture may be regarded as something of a status symbol, since the ownership of dovecotes was restricted to lords of manors, who might, of course, be either lay or monastic. For this reason they were unpopular with the peasantry, who complained that the rich were able to fatten their pigeons in fields which they themselves had the right to glean for their own winter grain.

For splendid dovecotes, which continued to be built until the feudal rights attached to them were abolished in the seventeenth century, we cannot do better than visit Daglingworth and Bibury to see cylindrical dovecotes, and Kelmscott Manor, William Morris's beautiful Cotswold home, which has a fine seventeenth-century dovecote and a barn with a pigeon-house in the gable. The Bibury dovecote has a lantern in the roof for pigeons to enter by, but this must have been a later edition.

Ducks became domesticated as farmyard birds at the same time as pigeons, and continue to be typical features of the Cotswold farmyard scene. In that invaluable family record J. Smythe's *Lives of the Berkeleys*, we learn that in the thirteenth century the reigning Lord Berkeley was receiving 288 ducks annually for the castle table.

On all their manors the Berkeleys built dovecotes in pleasances where peacocks strutted and displayed their plumage against walls of honey-coloured limestone. The Berkeleys also encouraged the keeping of bees for wax and honey, and in innumerable other ways started the civilized traditions which have continued to be part and parcel of Cotswold life for rich and poor. We get the feel of this Berkeley influence, and Cotswold feudal influence generally, in such villages as Bagendon, with beautiful old barns north and east of the little church with its saddle-backed tower, and Bibury, judged by William Morris to be the most beautiful village in England.

Bibury Court may be regarded as the ultimate achievement in Cotswold vernacular when seen in relation to Greville's Gothic house at Chipping Campden. Every element in Cotswold Tudor Gothic is present in Bibury Court: the array of gables capped with finials soaring up into steeply pitched roofs, the windows with narrow lights framed in stone mullions, and so forth. The porch is distinctively Jacobean, but it is in harmony with the Elizabethan features and, in its round-headed doorway, even harks back without incongruity to the Norman. Like all Tudor manor-houses in the Cotswolds, Bibury Court and Kelmscott Manor are indivisible from their farms. Of Kelmscott, William Morris wrote: that it was built 'of well-laid rubble stone of the district, the wall of the latter part being buttered over, so to say, with thin plaster which has now weathered to the same colour as the stone of the walls; the roofs are covered with the beautiful stone slates of the district, the most lovely covering which a roof can have'. The kitchen at Kelmscott is still called 'the Cheese Room'.

One of the principal charms of Cotswold farmsteads and manor-houses is the complete absence of any sense of superiority of one building over another. A pigsty is as dignified in style as a dovecote, a byre as a barn. All belong to Cotswold, with such practical distinctions as pigsties being enclosed with large flagstones to prevent the pigs nuzzling out stones and weakening the walls!

It would be pleasant to think that the Orders of nuns established in the region contributed to these gentler aspects of Cotswold life. The traditions of one nunnery are preserved in the name Minchinghampton, from the Old English *mynecen*, nun, where the abbess had seventeen hundred sheep grazing on vast commons and sheep-runs. South of the Cotswolds the nuns farmed so successfully that it was said that, 'If the Abbot of Glastonbury could marry the Abbess of Shaftesbury, their first-born would inherit more land than the King of England.' It must, however, be remembered that sheep were grazing on the Cotswolds long before the monks and nuns arrived. The element 'ship' in local place-names is evidence of their presence more than a thousand years ago, and the fulling-mill at Chedworth of clothmaking during the Roman Occupation.

What did not change in the Cotswold reputed transition from 'corn to sheep and from sheep to corn again' was the persistence of the medieval style of building which became most distinctive in the seventeenth century and which has remained so constant ever since that for some connoisseurs of building styles its charm may pall. In *Monmouthshire Houses** Sir Cyril Fox and Lord Raglan said: 'The formal and parallel verticalities of the Cotswold tradition seem, after a time, dull, because they are so obvious ... But,' they add, 'when they are flouted or ignored the result is disastrous.'

Far more than 'formal and parallel verticalities' went into the creation of the Cotswold tradition. Perhaps the distinctive elements are most concisely summed up at Postlip, where the monks of Winchcombe were responsible for the complete unity between the small Norman chapel (with seventeenth-century bellcote), manor-house and fourteenth-century tithe-barn, with north and south porches and ecclesiastical interior. The human figure so delicately carved in stone which stands on one of the gable ends is believed to represent the builder, and a local legend maintains that at a certain time of year it descends from its pedestal on hearing the midnight chimes of the chapel bell, to drink in the wishing-well below Cleeve.

Barns continue to dominate the domestic architecture of the Cotswolds, although from a utilitarian point of view they are now as obsolete as ploughs. They were approaching that assessment when, in the early years of the nineteenth century, the Board of Agriculture's most perceptive surveyor, William Marshall, wrote of their vast interiors: 'One foot below the beams is worth two above.' The best are actually off the Wolds, yet all are distinctively Cotswold in style: Great Coxwell, Bredon (now restored after a disastrous fire), Ashleworth, Hartpury, Frocester.

The tithe-barn of the Augustinian canons at Ashleworth, like the one at Hartpury, faces the church across the village green, again showing the importance of seeing Cotswold buildings in association with each other at the heart of practically every hamlet and village. Both Ashleworth and Hartpury have Cotswold style finials on the gables. The great barn at Frocester is 184 feet long, 30

*National Museum of Wales, three vols., 1951-54

Great Coxwell barn, Cotswold Stone

feet wide and 36 feet high to the roof ridge. The twelve-foot-high walls, built between 1264 and 1306, are supported by massive buttresses, required both to hold up the walls and to support the weight of the roof. The interior is ventilated by narrow slits between the buttresses. Bradford-on-Avon has a barn at Barton Farm, formerly a grange of the abbots of Shaftesbury, which the name suggests would be built as a barley barn. A magnificent barn at Tisbury, north-east of Shaftesbury, has thirteen bays and is four feet longer than the Frocester barn. The roofs of all these medieval barns are supported internally by cruck frames embedded in the walls, and beams and rafters supported by arcades of oak pillars, which means that they are really stone-clad timber-framed buildings. As their timbers are exposed, they are pattern-book studies of timber-framing over a period extending from the twelfth to the sixteenth century. The largest have gabled porches projecting midway along both the long sides lofty enough to allow carts to stand in while waiting to be unloaded, and like the great barn at Frocester, have slits in the masonry for ventilation.

Whatever their place in twentieth-century farming may be, as these great barns dominated farmsteads for six hundred years, to destroy them would be sacrilege. Similarly important barns may be found all along the stone belt extending from Dorset to the Wash, and on other downs and wolds, but there is no better place than a Cotswold barn in which to while away an hour dreaming about the scenes once witnessed in them. The doors were kept open while the harvested corn was threshed on the winnowing floor between them, so that the wind could blow through and separate the wheat from the chaff. When the threshing was done by hand, the clatter of flails being swung by the brawny arms of the farm bailiff and his labourers, squatting on the hard earthen floor, would be as familiar a country sound as that of tractors today.

Most Cotswold villages had their quarries, and immediately after harvest the men would go 'ridding' together – that is, taking off a thin layer of topsoil to get at the stone, which they would lift with a pick and leave on the surface to be 'frosted', which meant being split into slats or flags by the action of frost. The thicker of these could then be broken by the mere tap of a hammer into sizes suitable for drystone walling; the thinner were used for roofing, with the slats laid, like straw in thatching, with the heaviest at the bottom to support those of lighter weight above. The names given to these reflected the kind of country humour we find in the gargoyles that carry the rainwater off the roofs of churches: bachelors, short-backs, long-backs. Jenny-why-gettest-thou, rogue-why-winkest-thou?. In the same spirit, the upright stones along the tops of drystone walls were called toppers, cock-ups or combers, from their resemblance to the fleshy tufts on the heads of cocks.

The most famous quarries, from which the best roofing slats have come for centuries, are near Stow-in-the-Wold, especially those at Temple Guiting and Eyford. Only a limited number of quarries actually produce the fine-grained stone that can be cut with a saw.

Like all drystone walls, those in the Cotswolds derive their firmness from being wider at the bottom than at the top. The largest stones are laid as a base course to resist water seepage after a thin layer of soil has been removed to get a level trench, then each succeeding course is built slightly recessed from the one beneath it. The slope is correctly related to the height by having a wooden frame alongside the end, with a plummet-bob hanging down the middle. The effect of the stone being in layers makes the building

Farm with buildings grouped for shelter

of Cotswold walls much simpler than those of the Pennines, where the stones are blasted out of rock faces and tumble into heaps of every conceivable shape at the foot. Cotswold masons can build between twenty and thirty feet of wall, four feet high, in a single day with no other mechanical aid than a light-weight stone-hammer.

At Stow-on-the-Wold, 'where the wind blow cold', we realize why so many Cotswold farms are built in sheltered hollows, many of which may be abandoned quarries, and why they are all in a huddle with other farm buildings. A hill-top farmhouse may look splendid in the Kent or Sussex Weald. In the Cotswold it looks naked and exposed unless well protected from the prevailing winds

112

The Old Chapel, Walpole, Suffolk: this simple meeting-house, the oldest in the county, was built in 1607 as a village farmhouse. It was converted into a Nonconformist Chapel in 1647

Prouds Farm, Thaxted, Essex: a modernized farmhouse which retains the timbers of the medieval core of a typical Essex hall-house extended with gabled wings in the 16th and 17th centuries. The massive chimney stack asserts the claim of the occupier to yeoman status in the period of agricultural prosperity following the release from monastic control. Note the small windows under the eaves

Duck End, Great Dunmow, Essex: a typical home of a working Yeoman farmer in the rich, rolling countryside of north Essex

Great Tawney Hall, west Essex: it grew in stages from a small, timber-framed hall-house into a commodious double-pile farmhouse and finally acquired the handsome red-brick front with nine sash windows and a parapet to give it height, while leaving the weatherboard cladding of the original outshut undisguised

Manor Farm, Walkern, Hertfordshire: standing beside its pond, here is one of Hertfordshire's most delightful buildings. In the middle ages only abbeys and manors were legally permitted to have dovecotes. That at Walkern has recently been discreetly converted

Walker's Farm, Meesden, Hertfordshire: thatched and timber-framed, this small farmhouse is representative of those still to be found in parts of east Hertfordshire and in Essex

Dragons Green, Benington, Hertfordshire: now a mauve-coloured private residence, this house has in its time been the Green Dragon pub and Shenley Farm. Note the neatly-executed capping of the thatch

The Olde House, Harrietsham, Kent: formerly known as Old Bell Farm, this is an outstanding example of a Wealden-type house and dates from at least the 16th century. Much of the fabric remains in its original form. Features to note include the lower courses of scalloped roof tiles, the central coving, and the ancient front door and doorcase

Corner Farm, Langley, Kent: whereas The Olde House, Harrietsham, remains largely unaltered, Corner Farm has been restored so that open hall and tall windows again conform to the general style of a Wealden house

Malt House Farm, Egerton, Kent: embodies timber-framing and tile-hanging typical of the county. A reminder that farmers in various parts of Britain often used to pursue an additional occupation such as brewing, fishing, or mining

The Plestor, near Borden, Kent: showing the handmade roof tiles, brick-work, white-painted weatherboarding, and flint walling characteristic of buildings in Kent

Brockwells Farm, near Isfield, East Sussex: a typical Sussex farmhouse of brick and hung tiles standing end on to the road

Boathouse Farm, Isfield, East Sussex: despite its name this brick and tilehung farmhouse lies almost half a mile from the Sussex River Ouse

Church Farm, Fletching, East Sussex: an 18th-century chequered brick-work farmhouse at the back of which may be seen a little timber-framing of earlier date

Sheep House Farm, near Coln St Dennis, Gloucestershire: the name of this relatively modern farmhouse, near the old Salt Way, is a reminder of the source of the wealth that produced the 'wool churches' of the Cotswolds and the typically 'Gothic' style of the domestic architecture

by trees, which, as in other exposed districts, tend to be beeches, while in the valleys chestnuts are favoured for farmyards, with variety introduced by grey-green yews in neighbouring church-yards.

The need for sheltered sites, combined with the enduring quality of Cotswold stone, has meant that the villages have retained their farmsteads. Most of the farmhouses were originally longhouses but, although they began in the usual way with stock and family under a single-storeyed building, they have often evolved in individual ways. Whereas the extensions in most parts of the country developed with the early addition of a lean-to, called an outshut, under a 'catslide' roof at the rear, the weight of Cotswold stone roofing was so great that the first additions were often at right angles to the original building, under a separate roof. The rear walls of these outshuts might later be adapted for use as lean-to sheds for carts, or even as stables. In larger farmsteads they might take the form of projecting wings at the end of farmhouses, which, where there was a two-storeyed porch midway along the front, resulted in E-shaped buildings. Courtyard farmsteads are found, but they are much rarer in the Cotswolds than in more fertile Midlands counties.

The confined space available in the wolds led to greater ingenuity being exercised than in flat country south of the Fosse Way, where the courtyard plan did evolve. Nevertheless, in the hills a farmstead might be built on the southern slopes and extended in the manner characteristic of the Pennines. Where this was done, the end portions might be left single-storeyed while the house-part in the middle was being built with a gabled upper storey, which might later be given a third storey with attics lighted by windows in the gables. It seems reasonable to believe that the Cotswold custom of building up roof gables flush with the lower walls, instead of insetting them as dormers, was to gain additional support for the weight of the roof. Many of the attics in large farmhouses are found to be single large rooms, suggesting that some of them may have been used for weaving or spinning as well as for storage.

The flooring of Cotswold farmhouses used to be an interesting study. Earth floors were common, as they were everywhere. In the South of England tiles were laid flat on them from the sixteenth century; in the Cotswolds, as in the North of England, they were paved with flagstones; but these were not usually of limestone. They were of blue lias, which may still be seen through the open doors of cottages on Cotswold village streets.

South-east of the Fosse as it crosses the region, the scene changes. The soil is fertile and dairy-farming flourishes. Cirencester, the Corinium Dobunnorum of the Romans, with defences enclosing 240 acres, is still the capital. It was from his home in the valley of the Upper Thames that William Morris, born in the year in which Cobbett died, saw the Cotswolds with less bullish eyes. He admired the churches as everyone must, but to him the thirteenth-century tithe-barn at Great Coxwell, now in the care of the National Trust, was one of the noblest buildings in England, and out of his excited admiration for the Cotswold heritage in stone the Society for the Protection of Ancient Buildings was founded, with himself as its first secretary. In the cause of conservation he was followed in 1902 by C.R. Ashbee's guild of local craftsmen.

The early accession of wealth to the Cotswolds from the sale of wool by the Church and the great manorial families gave the region its own distinctive church architecture during the fifteenth century. During the sixteenth, by an inspired instinct, the lords of manors who were building farmhouses took the proportions and basic design for these from the churches, employing, no doubt, master masons descended from those who had built them and had learned their craft at Gloucester or Bristol. They would recognize that such ornate features as those on churches like Chipping Campden or Northleach would be inappropriate for farmhouses. So they evolved a style of domestic architecture with a communal unity of design in which, although nothing dominates, everything has grace and dignity, barn, byre, inn and manor-house standing in relaxed good-neighbourliness with every other building.

So when towards the end of Elizabeth's reign the rest of England began rebuilding its farmhouses, those in the Cotswold were still sound, and their style, with stone mullioned window-frames under square dripstones, flagstone roofs broken by dormers or gables, and low porches, was firmly established. The indoor timbers were still invariably of native oak, split by axe and trimmed by adze. But inevitably some did fall into disrepair and had to be rebuilt or refurbished. When this happened, it was still unthinkable that any

114

other style should be introduced – no doubt 'Cotsall style' was the only style known to country masons in Stow-on-the-Wold or Northleach at that time. For local historians this may make dating difficult from outdoor evidence. Fortunately, county record offices have been established throughout England during the last fifty years, and estate records have been deposited in them. They are of inestimable value and are the foundation of much of the work being done by scholars engaged on that great enterprise *'The Victoria History of the Counties of England*. From these studies in Gloucestershire, we now know that the great rebuilding period in the Cotswolds and along the Welsh Marches did not come until the period from the Restoration of Charles II in 1660 to about 1725.

There are three regions in England which produced outstandingly distinctive styles during the late seventeenth-century building boom: the West Midlands in ornate timber-framing, East Anglia in flint combined with brick, and the Cotswolds in stone. There were economic reasons for this which were common to all three. The wool boom was over, and countrymen had to look for new sources of prosperity. As so often happens, human greed had outstripped the means for gratifying itself. The danger of this happening had been foreseen in 1533, when Henry VIII decreed that no wool-farmer should keep more than two thousand sheep. Again, as so often happens, the proposed remedy was too simple. It failed to recognize the complexity of the problem. But in the Cotswolds, where dependence on sheep had been greater than in most parts, it did impose restrictions on enterprise in the north of the district, and although in the lowlands south-west of the Fosse there was no difficulty in readjusting the economy, the strength of tradition was so strong that the new farmhouses continued to be built in the old style, and any modifications were evolutionary rather than revolutionary. There are few buildings with expanded upper storeys supported on jetties, which is an Elizabethan innovation in most parts of the South.

Probably the characteristic which strikes most tourists in the Cotswolds is the building up of part of the front wall into gables which break the line of the eaves. This meant that the device employed in the South-West and North-West of building external chimneystacks to avoid weakening the walls was not necessary, so central chimneystacks became common, and new farmhouses could be built two rooms deep if desired, with fireplaces back to back in them. Most of these two-room-deep farmhouses are, as one might expect, south of the Fosse.

Rise in status is shown most obviously in porches. The earliest form of protecting outer doors was for two flagstones to be arranged as a hood over the front door, but as ecclesiastical architects had proclaimed importance the world over by building stately porches, domestic architecture in the Cotswolds evolved a Gothic style of porch for farmhouses, with moulded jambs, arched head and perhaps a date-stone bearing the initials of the builder.

This perfection in detail was the more easily achieved because the structural lines were simple and directed to nothing more complicated than good proportions, which became instinctive to every competent master mason. It is this basic simplicity that continues to make Cotswold style so appropriate, with minor variations, to every kind of local building, from a medieval church and barn to the typical eighteenth-century civic building and manor-house. For many of us it symbolizes the ideal architectural relationship which exists in the English parish between the land and the men and women who got every basic need from it.

In personalizing buildings, door-hoods were popular with enterprising masons for the scope they provided for advertising their skill. There are so many in Chipping Campden that one suspects they were selected from pattern-books, but in most villages the interest may be in recognizing the 'house styles' of long-established mason families. Many farmhouse porches and window heads were obviously derived from the mouldings of the square-headed windows that came into use for churches during the Tudor period, and from manor-houses. A favourite feature is the pineapple finial seen on a farmhouse on the outskirts of Chipping Campden, carved with a skill that may be recognized on several cottages and supremely in the finials of the eight gables of the frontage of the almshouses.

The rebuilding that transformed farmhouses in the more prosperous parts of the Cotswolds after the Restoration of Charles II in 1660 provided an opportunity to correct a not uncommon defect in earlier planning: the building of farmhouses with their backs to the sun, which was thought too injurious to household furnishings to be welcomed. It did not correct all defects. None of the seventeenth-century farmhouses had damp courses. Later – much later – larger farmhouses were given cavity walls and modern flooring, but the stone mullioned windows, with their diamond-shaped lattices and wrought-iron hinges, were almost invariably retained. At Ebrington, near Burford, new houses were being built in the old style in the nineteenth century. One noteworthy feature of the late seventeenth-century farmhouses was the addition of a projecting porch, with a room for storing fleeces or farm produce above it, rising to a third gable.

These village farmhouses reflect the difference in prosperity between the lowlands and the hills. Research on the local families of master masons has probably already been done by local historians. If not, it would be well worth undertaking. There must be ample material for it available in estate papers deposited in county records offices. Such features as the different sizes and positioning of gables and dormers must have been the 'trade marks' of different families.

An enormous amount of research has been done on Cotswold buildings and will continue to be done. The subject is inexhaustible. But it is not a subject for scholars only. We can all appreciate the way the patina of age has descended on them from the lichens that settle on the rough, uneven texture of the roof slats, the play of light daily to be witnessed on the steeply pitched roofs enlivened by tiny dormers like those at Bibury, the well-carved finials that break the lines of the overhanging eaves, the welcoming porches and the beautiful texture of the oolitic limestone that sparkles so brightly in the sun. All these contribute to the charm of Cotswold Gothic. No matter how haphazard the arrangement of either farm or cottage groupings may appear to be, they have an unselfconscious unity and an elegant simplicity unmatched elsewhere. The style continues throughout most of Oxfordshire and parts of Northamptonshire. Similar vernacular styles were evolved by farmer-masons, or estate masons, in Dorset and the Yorkshire Pennines. But there is a professional element in the domestic architecture of the Cotswolds which can only be attributed to the persisting influence of the schools of masons trained to build churches and tithe-barns for the wealthy monastic landowners. So the Cotswold scene remains as William Marshall described it, with the final comment: 'The eye must be dim, and the heart benumbed, which can be insensible to the rural beauty of Cotswold.'

8. Northern Pastoral

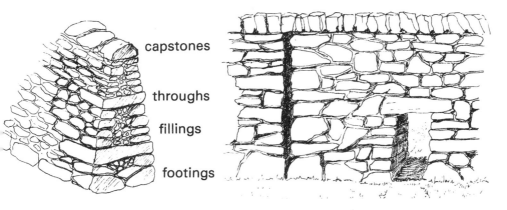

capstones

throughs

fillings

footings

Northern pastoral drystone walling

The distinctively northern scenery of England starts in the Peak district of Derbyshire, the first region to be designated a National Park. The south-western Peak borders the Potteries, the northern is within reach of Sheffield in the east and Manchester and Liverpool in the west. But between sombre areas of Carboniferous limestone and heavy industry, the inner Peak is a place of gritstone hills and sheltered valleys through which trout streams run to water a landscape that has nothing in common with the downland of the south, everything in common with the pastoral Pennines of the north.

With good stone at hand in their own quarries, the landowners of the Peak were able to build farmhouses that are as characteristic as the churches of local style: long, low buildings with wide-gabled façades and other features reminiscent of the Cotswolds. Like the Cotswold gables, those in Derbyshire run up through the eaves without a break from the lower walls, but they are wider and lower than the Cotswold gables, as a result of the roofs being less steeply pitched. In short, they reflect Welsh influence but are typically northern in their bluntness. Among the best old houses is sixteenth-century Bradbourne Hall, where the Bradbourne family were already seated as landowners in the thirteenth century. Lea Hall, where the cornmill is still in working order, is another old home of the Bradbournes. There must be more than fifty cornmills in and around the Peak.

It is extremely unlikely that the old farmhouses of the North were ever like those of the Cotswolds in being Gothic in style. The dominant monastic influence was Cistercian, and the Cistercians built churches like barns rather than barns like churches. The first had low, drystone walls, in which cruck frames were embedded to support roofs of turf and bracken, often referred to in records as 'black thatch'. Alongside them, other drystone walls enclosed small fields called garths, like those still to be seen at Malham, which were built as folds for sheep brought down from Malham Moor in bad weather, and crofts for a few Celtic short-horned cattle. Pigs fattened on acorns and beech-nuts in the shaws and cloughs of the fellside gills. Poultry were abundant. Many of the cottages on the Duke of Devonshire's estates at Bolton Abbey in Yorkshire were single-storeyed, cruck-framed and ling-thatched until the early years of the nineteenth century, as were the cottages at Hawes and throughout Wensleydale, where the Corporation of London formerly owned estates. There is a document in the Corporation archives recording that when in 1652 commissioners were appointed to negotiate the sale of these Wensleydale estates, they reported that the tenants had 'for the most part houses no better than their cowhouses, built without mortar or loam'.* North Country drystone walling would inevitably appear more primitive to southern eyes than to northern.

There are farmhouses on the fells along the Lancashire-Yorkshire border which retained direct communication between family and livestock quarters until well within living memory, and Kepp House, Burton-in-Lonsdale, retains evidence of doors giving access from the kitchen into the 'fodder-gang' of the cowshed, so called because it was the passage (gangway) along which fodder was delivered to the cattle stalls.

*Corp. of London. Proc. of the Royal Estates Comm. vol. 11, 113-14.

According to the economic historian Gregory King, the seven northern counties of Derbyshire, Cheshire, Lancashire, Yorkshire, Cumberland, County Durham and Northumberland were the poorest in England even at the end of the seventeenth century. But like their Herdwick sheep, northern farmers had learned to survive on poor pasturage and had evolved a way of life that had many compensations. Until recently few farms in hill country were of more than a hundred acres, although having grazing rights on the fells, but they were family farms, and as all the families in a dale were related, the entire population was an extended family in which every member felt free to call on any other member in an emergency.

The abbeys owned most of the land in the Middle Ages, and the habits of thrift and hard work which remain characteristics of the northerner were inculcated by Cistercian monks who had studied Roman writers on agriculture and knew a great deal about breeding. An admirable example of their training methods was given as evidence at the Dissolution by a shepherd on Fountains Fell in Gigglewick, Yorkshire, who said that he had been given a lamb by his Cistercian employers as part of his wages at the end of his first year of service, and when the abbey estates were redistributed that lamb had produced for him three score and thirteen good ewes. Hence, incidentally, the northern system of tenancy, in which when a farm changes hands a stipulated flock goes with it.

Flagstones must have superseded thatch in most parts of the north early. There is an intriguing reference in the Ripon records of a William Sclater selling to the cathedral chapter a thousand slate stones in 1399,* and in his *History of Craven* Dr Whitaker describes Appletreewick Hall as being a slated house rebuilt in the fourteenth century. Other pointers to flagstones replacing thatch early are low-pitched roofs being so universal in the 1580-1650 rebuilding, since thatch requires a steeper pitch to allow rainwater to run off quickly, and the entire lack of hipped roofs in old houses in the western dales. Otherwise Yorkshire farmhouses have many features in common with those of Dorset. The chimneystacks are

---

*Memorials of Ripon, Surtees Society, 111, p.130

squat in both, the gable ends plain. The stone mullions framing the windows are similar but with the difference that it is usual for the windows to slide sideways in Yorkshire instead of pointing out on wrought-iron hinges. The larger halls in both have wide-gabled wings and two-storeyed porches. Simple finials at the peaks and angles of the front walls are common features. But the most prominent feature is the heavy front door, usually painted white and studded with square-headed nails painted black. A wide lintel, often with dripstones, surmounts it, giving prominence to a tablet bearing the initials of the builder – sometimes with those of his wife, and the date of the buildings. These inscriptions are so individually designed that one could probably say that no two are identical.

A characteristic northern feature that was unknown before the sixteenth century is the ubiquitous sycamore, which now provides shelter, or bield, to every fellside farmstead. To Gerard it was the great maple. As soil with plenty of lime in it suits the sycamore, it quickly colonized the cloughs, and as manure also suits it, the sycamore became the farmstead tree after the 1580-1650 rebuilding, when shippons were built for the cows that had become more profitable than sheep. These shippons were built at the end of the longhouses where the land sloped away, so that the slurry could be carried off. Today solitary clumps of sycamores on fellsides often indicate the sites of demolished farmsteads of which every vestiage has disappeared because the stone has been used for other buildings.

In areas where the farmhouse only was rebuilt in the 1580-1650 boom, the character of the original house can often be deduced from ancillary buildings. For example, the timber-framed barn at East Riddleston Hall, Keighley, suggests that the original farmhouse was timber-framed when Camden described the family as the most prolific in England, alleging that in 1555, when Christopher Metcalfe met the judges at York, 'he was attended by three hundred horsemen, all of his own name and kindred, well mounted and suitably attired.' There are still many timber-framed farmhouses with halls open to the roof, flanked by two-storeyed wings, in the rolling countryside of the Yorkshire Wolds, where rich corn-producing valleys continue to be tilled and pedigree stock is reared, on the great estates of the Halifax, Sykes, Normanby and Worsley families.

In those eastern parts of Yorkshire signs of the influence of settlers from the Low Countries are everywhere, even in such industrial regions as the ancient parish of Halifax, where old houses in streets, although externally seventeenth-century, on examination are found to be farmhouses with struts and beams of Tudor oak at the core and only encased in stone. Huddersfield and Dewsbury have similar yeoman-clothier houses, now restored by well-to-do wool merchants with no connection with the land. There are houses of the same character in Lancashire but there was always more money to be made out of wool than out of cotton.

Most of the farmhouses on the eastern side of the Craven Gap in Yorkshire are built of Carboniferous limestone, with small windows for defence against the weather. Most of those on the western side were formerly on the estates of Fountains Abbey, and later of families as powerful as the Cliffords, which produced that great lady Anne Clifford, Countess of Pembroke and Montgomery, whose influence may be looked for around her castle at Skipton. They are of limestone rubble laid in courses and plastered. The surrounding countryside is brighter and softer, with green pastures lush from the wetter climate. They have orchards with apple and damson trees, gooseberry bushes and honeysuckle over the roof of a privy in a corner of the garden, which sometimes has two seats side by side! The number of place-names containing 'apple' and 'plum' testifies to fruit having been grown here time out of mind. Crab-apples and damsons must surely be natives. A supper at the end of hay-harvest without apple pie would be unthinkable.

To the west of Skipton is the ancient Forest of Bowland, now in Lancashire, watered by the rivers Ribble and Hodder which flow through dales as fertile as the valleys in the foothills of the Delamere Forest in Cheshire. Many of the farmhouses were manor-houses with names in which 'hall' is as common as 'grange' is in the Peak. The medieval difference between the two is illustrated by the fact that most of the granges in the Peak were outlying manors of monastic orders; most of the halls in Bowland were built by such ancient families as the Asshetons of Downham, the Lysters of Middop, the Parkers of Browsholme, the Hackings,

Shuttleworths and Walmesleys, who built Hacking Hall, and whose descendants are still farming at Mitton. Most of the really ancient families – the Sherburnes, Trappes-Lomaxes, Welds and a score of others of less note were Roman Catholic and played prominent parts in the Pilgrimage of Grace. On the whole they were families of simple dignity and courage rather than of great wealth, although the Sherburnes were outstanding exceptions as their monument in the Roman Catholic college at Stonyhurst and their tombs in Mitton church prove. The halls of these families were rebuilt in stone at the end of the sixteenth or beginning of the seventeenth century. Little Mearley Hall on Pendle side was one of the first, dating from 1590, Browsholme 1605-10, Hacking 1607.

After Browsholme, the farmhouse most remarkably well preserved in Bowland is Bashall Hall, built by the Talbots, which retains the galleries where retainers were quartered above the stables. Browsholme, the home of the Parkers, is the showpiece of the Hodder Valley, full of mementoes collected by distinguished antiquaries and scholars of the family which produced a humane and far-sighted Lord Chief Justice in the present century. Waddington Old Hall has been well restored, and every parish has farmhouses dating from the reigns of Elizabeth I and James I. Architectural historians repeatedly tell us how far the North was behind the South in adopting new building styles, yet all the halls and farmhouses just mentioned belong to the great period of rebuilding already mentioned several times. The oriels and tall mullioned and transomed windows at Bashall cannot be much later than the best in the whole of the stone belt which runs transversely across England from Dorset to Yorkshire. The conservative styling springs not from ignorance but from the innate steadfastness of men who like to live as their fathers lived.

The truth is that within a remarkably short period following the Dissolution Yorkshire had become surpremely the county of landed gentry and yeoman farmers. Though Cobbett said he found Suffolk farmers great boasters, adding that their boasts were not without justification, the same could be said of Yorkshiremen. I remember a grand old Yorkshire lady replying with pride when I expressed sympathy on the death of her yeoman husband: 'Aye, we breed good men as well as good horses in Yorkshire.'

A good place to see farmhouses that were formerly manor-houses of the farming gentry and breeders of prize-winning stallions are the roads from Stokesley through Bilsdale to Helmsley, and between Thirsk and Pickering. This is an accurate and most sensitive description of one such farmhouse in Sir Herbert Read's memories of his childhood home in this part of Yorkshire in *Annals of Innocence and Experience* (1940).

But while there is wide variety in the farmhouses of this largest of English counties, there is one distinctive type in the dales and on the fells of Yorkshire called the lathe-house, from the Old Scandinavian word for barn. In the Cotswolds and West Midlands provision could be made for the storage of crops in granaries that might stand away from the house or be tucked in at the rear. On the northern fells, where winters are severe and the most valuable livestock is on the hills, families and stock continue to live under one roof in longhouse style, but the roof is extended to incorporate a barn between the shippon and the house.

To understand the fell farmer's attachment to the lathe-house it is only necessary to spend a few nights in one in mid-winter, when the wind is howling and the snow drifting perilously. At such times it is a great comfort to the farmer and his family, lying snugly in their beds, to hear the quiet lowing of beasts in the byre, or the clatter of hoofs on the cobbles of the stable floor as a horse rises from his bed of bracken to answer the whinny of a mare on a farm half a mile away. The animals share in this sense of security, as well as in the warmth that circulates from one end of the building to the other.

Two fine old lathe-houses in the Dales impressed me so much during a walking tour more than fifty years ago that they have remained in my memory ever since. One is Newhouse Farm, the other Dale Foot, both built in the first half of the seventeenth century and both in Bishopdale. Another farmhouse that returns to mind when Yorkshire is mentioned is Nunnery Farm, Arthington (1583), which can be seen from the road between Otley and Harewood and is remarkable for the astonishingly large number of its stone-mullioned windows. It is a feature of Yorkshire farmhouses that, although there is common style, with mullions and dripstones, the number of lights may be varied.

125

Nunnery farmhouse, Arthington, North Yorkshire

The need to incorporate. barns in longhouses came with the livestock expansion through organized cattle-breeding at the end of the Middle Ages. Before that, there had been little need to store crops, since sheep fend for themselves. The movement in Yorkshire was led by the monks of Fountains Abbey, near Ripon. At the Dissolution, the inventory made of the abbey's possessions listed on the demesne lands 2,356 head of cattle against 1,326 sheep. In this impressive total there were herds of milk cows to the number of 738 – and this long before the industrial towns of the north had sprung up to provide ready markets for the sale of milk and dairy produce. No doubt the explanation is found in the fact that, when Fountains was in its glory, dairy produce – mainly, no doubt, in the form of cheese – was sold for export to the Continent. From the Records of Fountains we may deduce that Wensleydale cheese had been known for four hundred years prior to the Dissolution. At the end of the twelfth century there were probably more than fifty monks and at least two hundred lay brothers working on the abbey's estates. With such a landowner, the farmhouses built on estates brought up to such a level of productivity before the monks were succeeded by the yeomen could not be other than they are.

These cattle ranches, if we may call them that, were mainly in the fertile valleys east of the Pennines and the Craven Gap, where the lay-out of the villages testifies to the persistence of Anglo-Saxon traditions in predominantly Scandinavian settlements, which on this side of the Pennines were Danish. These settlements, incidentally, account for the complexity of the names still used for cowhouses in the North. In Craven they are called shippons, in Nidderdale mistals, in the Halifax district boosies, and in the Dales that run down from Stainmore into Teesdale they are called byres. Anyone wishing to make a study of these names might start with 'The Wife of Bath's Tale', in which Chaucer calls them 'shepenes'.

The greatest transformation in farm buildings within living memory has been in the rebuilding of shippons and the production of milk generally. There can be no regrets about the disappearance of the old custom of milking while squatting on a three-legged stool with one's head resting on the cow's flank. I wonder if this need to press the forehead against the cow was due to the soporific effect of the rhythmic sound of the milk as it hissed into the pail gripped between the milker's knees. When the pail was full, it was either carried from the shippon into the dairy, to be deposited on the flag floor against the whitewashed wall and another pail taken, or emptied into a milk kit by the shippon door. Conditions are very different now, and the transformation came none too soon for the health of the nation.

Dairies were already fully hygienic. The 'working tops' and shelves were hugh slabs of blue slate from local quarries. There was a famous quarry at Helwith Bridge producing them and another at Lawkland, which also specialized in roofing slates. The placing of cleanliness below godliness never made sense to a true-hearted Yorkshire farmer's wife. To her cleanliness *was* godliness. You never congratulated her on her cooking. The excellence of that was taken for granted. Her pride was in keeping her floor so clean that you said you could eat off it.

Farmhouse dairies are still nostalgic places for those who were brought up in days when butter was made in them regularly. The milk was left to 'set' in shallow pans. The cream was then skimmed off with shells or shallow saucers in a slow process that tickled the taste-buds of those who wanted cream with everything – hence the expression 'creamed-off' for any process that takes away the valuable part and offers for sale what is worthless. But as with every other laborious process, means had to be found to relieve the farmer's wife and her maids of the drudgery of working the churn. Two dogs were placed on the wheel with their collars strapped to the beam. When the churn was ready, the beam was given a sharp starting turn, and the dogs had to run hard to keep upright as the wheel turned. It sounds cruel to us now, but we are assured that the dogs barked merrily and had every appearance of enjoying themselves. When the butter came, the wheel began to bump clumsily and the dogs were released. Dog wheels were succeeded by a rocking contrivance worked by donkeys, the tread of the donkey working the rocker.

When farmhouse dairies were at the height of their pride, butter was moulded in round wooden bowls with an individual stamp either on the base of the bowl or on the lid. These neatly carved stamps – emblems of the farms that took great pride in the presentation of their butter – were succeeded by corrugated handboards used for patting the butter into the prosaic brick shapes we now take off supermarket shelves with only a label for identification. A special farmhouse delicacy from the dairy that is still with us is beesting – the word was used by the Anglo-Saxons fifteen hundred years ago as *bysting*, 'thick milk', for the first milk drawn from the cow after calving. It was used to make custards and curd tarts.

Before cheeses were mass-produced for sale in supermarkets, every farmhouse of any size had a dairy making them, each claiming a distinctive flavour. In Wensleydale the local cheese derived its taste from the cows browsing in spring on the fresh green leaves of the alders that grew along the banks of the becks. Winter-made cheese, called 'hay-cheese', was said to be good enough only for Lancashire folk to make 'Welsh rabbit' with, which was grossly unfair, since the loose-textured Lancashire cheese, like Cheshire, has a special delicacy of its own.

The hams, wrapped in muslin, that hung from dairy ceilings

were very different from the tinned 'York Hams' that can be bought in any supermarket today. Real Yorkshire ham is cured like bacon, fried like bacon and served with eggs. It is cut from a ham that has a bloom on it, hanging from a beam in the kitchen to which it has been brought from the dairy, and ideally it is eaten in the kitchen. Its smooth, rich taste is derived from the meal, buttermilk and potato peelings on which the pig was fed before being killed, and to be at its best it should be hung for at least three months in a warm, well-ventilated kitchen before being eaten.

Until recently the English have had a poor reputation for cooking. Those responsible for this slanderous nonsense can never have fed on farmhouse fare in farmhouse kitchens or their words would have stuck in their gullets and choked them. Real apple pie, for example, could never be on speaking terms with the tablet of pastry with a dab of apple alongside it, the two never having come together before they met on the plate. Apparently there are compilers of guides to restaurants and hostels serving good food who do not know that apple pie, like any other pie, is baked in a dish with a complete lid of pastry.

No doubt the Yorkshireman's taste for cheese with everything seems as odd to Cornishmen as the Cornishman's taste for cream seems to Yorkshiremen. Apple pie, currant cake and mince pies are all eaten with cheese in Yorkshire, and bacon is fried and served with a slab of cheese toasted on top.

> A mince pie without the cheese
> Is like a kiss without the squeeze.

Then there is that other Yorkshire delicacy, curd cheese cakes, which must not be thought of as merely Bakewell tarts without the jam. Yorkshire curd cake is made by spreading the mixture over pastry in a tin six inches in diameter and baking it for half an hour. Everybody knows about Yorkshire pudding, but only Yorkshiremen know the richness of a hunk of Yorkshire parkin with a lump of cheese to finish off a meal. The true Yorkshire parkin is made of oatmeal and treacle and should be broken from a slab two to three inches thick served on the table. Traditionally it was served round the bonfire on 5 November. As to Yorkshire pudding, not everybody knows that it should always be served hot from the oven, or that there are two kinds, one thin, the other thick, but both like hot cake, crisp at the edges.

Another North Country delicacy was rum butter. To produce it, a dab of butter was placed in a brass pan and just sufficient heat applied to melt it. This resulted in the salt in the butter sinking to the bottom of the pan, leaving the milk to be skimmed off and the butter decanted free of salt. This was then beaten up with a quantity of sugar and rum, and flavoured with a little grated nutmeg already prepared in readiness. When the approved consistency had been reached, it was potted for production on special occasions and regular get-togethers, which, when families were large and all lived within reach of each other, were frequent and regular during the course of the year. For one of these, Mothering Sunday, simnel cakes were baked.

The heart of every farmhouse was the kitchen! The fire never went out and the women battled their way cheerfully through the household chores, defying the mockery of the cuckoo-clock from morning to night. There is an admirable description of a North Yorkshire yeoman's farm kitchen in *A Memorial of Cowgill Chapel* (1868) by Adam Sedgwick of Dent, who became an eminent Cambridge geologist: 'From one side of the fireplace ran a bench, with a strong and sometimes ornamentally carved back, called a long settle. On the other side of the fireplace was the Patriarch's wooden and well-carved arm-chair; and near the chair was the sconce adorned with crockery. Not far off was commonly seen a well-carved cupboard, or cabinet, marked with some date that fell within a period of fifty years after the Restoration of Charles II. One or two small tables, together with chairs and benches, gave seats to all the party assembled. ...' The 'well-carved cupboard' originated as a partition separating the living-room from the chamber or parlour. When interior walls were built, they became free-standing pieces of furniture, but on careful examination of the sides and back of early Tudor survivors, marks may be found as evidence of their having been incorporated in wattle-and-daub walls into which they had been pressed into position before the daub had dried.

Grandfather clocks, bible boxes, warming-pans and corner cupboards marked stages in the family's progress until they became

Cooking range in the Yorkshire Dales

essential furnishings, but the hearth was the heart of the home. By Adam Sedgwick's time the open fireplaces with the fire on the hearth, which are now being opened up again, would be filled in by a kitchen range with a deep grate for burning any kind of fuel, which in Yorkshire was usually peat. These grates were made by local blacksmiths and fixed between stone hobs. In less remote dales cast-iron ovens with side boilers had come into use towards the end of the eighteenth-century and continued to be universal in style until well into the present century, with steel fenders in front to protect the 'peg rugs', made of scraps of gaily coloured material pegged into hessian backs during winter evenings. These grates were labour-consuming but they were every housewife's pride and remarkably effective for every domestic purpose. If a good fire was kept going, the oven was hot all day, and cakes, Yorkshire

131

puddings, scones and batches of bread would be baked in succession to feed large households of family and servants. Most of these ranges have now been superseded by closed ranges, such as 'Rayburns', or by electric cookers. Early this century the hearthstones were damped with milk to darken them and then decorated with designs traced on them with sandstone.

There might be a gun rack in the chimney corner; there was always a salt box nailed to the wall. Now the familiar objects of sixty years ago are collectors' pieces, and old wills are searched for the traditional names of farmhouse bygones. A trough for kneading dough, like the one in the church at Alfriston in Sussex, was a 'kneadinge kymnell'. Bread in those days was baked in small, flat loaves on a 'griddle plate', an iron disc up to two feet in diameter.

An inner door led from the kitchen into the dairy, where jugs of cream stood on slate slabs, and butter in large wooden bowls. Nearly everything moveable in dairies was wooden and well scrubbed in those days. The exceptions were the large earthenware urns in which eggs were preserved. Oatmeal porridge, oatcake, hasty pudding, clapbread and riddle-cakes were daily fare in the Dales, with oats the staple diet because oats can tolerate a wetter climate than wheat can. Dr T.D. Whitaker in his *History of Craven* (1805) records of the dales folk that oats 'formed the principal article of their subsistence'. The kiln in which the grain was dried – Dr Whitaker's word was 'parched' – before being ground 'belonged to the township at large, and when in use was a sort of village coffee-house where the politics of the place and the day were discussed'.

The form of oatcake called clap-bread was so called because the cakes were clapped out by hand on a concave board. Real oatcake was made by rolling out a stiff paste of oatmeal poured onto a square or round stone or iron plate called a bakstone. With plenty of butter it was delicious eaten warm and was always brought to the table wrapped in a white tea-cloth. Another form, sometimes called riddlebread, was made from butter poured or thrown onto the bakstone. In the northern dales oatcake was called 'haverbread' from the old Norse *hafre*, oats, or 'girdlecake', because it was baked on a circular iron plate, or griddle. Clapbread was probably the early form of oatcake but it took more time to make than the common form. Celia Fiennes described the method perfectly in her own simple language after visiting the north in 1698:

> They mix their flour with water so soft as to rowle it in their hands in a ball, and then they have a board made round and something hollow in the middle riseing by degrees all round to the edge a little higher, but so little as one would take it to be only a board warp'd, this is to cast out the cake thinn and so they clap it round and drive it to the edge in a due proportion till drove as thinn as paper, and still they clap it and drive it round, and then they have a plaite of iron same size with their clap board and so shove off the cake on it and so set it on coales and bake it ... if their iron plaite is smooth and they take care their coales or embers are not too hot but just to make it look yellow, it will bake and be as crisp and pleasant to eate as anything you can imagine.*

The 'coles' were, of course, charcoal.

Oatcake is seldom seen on tables south of Scotland and the north of England now except in good hotels, where it is served with fresh salmon or prawns. The bakstones I remember were built in. They were square iron plates fired from below like old-fashioned washing boilers. There is one from a farm at Cartmel in the Museum of Lakeland Life and Industry at Kendal.

The 'well-carved cupboard' referred to by Adam Sedgwick was originally the 'bread cupboard', in which sufficient oatcake and other basic food might be stored to keep the family going for weeks in bad weather. Later they were used for storing family silver. In my family they were called court cupboards, perhaps because they had formerly screened off a private part of the hall or kitchen before interior walls were built. There were many instances in both sacred and secular literature of sanctums being called courts. Such mysteries are still unending. Why, as another example, should bins in which meal is stored, as well as the elaborately carved chests that descend in families as heirlooms, be called 'arks'? In this case, no doubt the simple answer is that the word is derived from the latin *arca*, a chest.

Probably few of us would want to return to the lives our grandparents lived – good as they appear in retrospect. But in memory the sights, sounds and smells we grew up with remain

*C. Morris, *The Journals of Celia Fiennes*, 1947. pp. 193-4

nostalgic to the end of our lives: the clack of the latch, the clatter of pans, the sharp click of approaching footsteps that caused the collie on the hearthrug to prick his ears for a moment before nosing down again among the pegged clippings on recognizing them as his master's. At night the kitchen was silent as though itself at rest, except for the steady tick of the case-clock. But outside there were the nightly sounds of cattle lowing in the far pasture, sheep bleating on the fells, and the familiar hooting of owls. Somehow all these sounds were sleep-inducing, and the household would be undisturbed until at dawn the entire small world would reawaken to the crowing of cocks and the neighing of horses as the clogs of the farmhands clattered across the farmyard cobbles to the stable door.

9. *Farmsteads of Cumbria and the Scottish Border*

Fellside farm, above Ambleside

Wordsworth's *Guide to the Lake Counties*, first published in 1810 and revised and reissued five times during his lifetime, was written to disabuse the public of the nonsense in 'Guides' providing superficial information for the new public of 'sentimental travellers', emboldened by improvements in transport to venture 'into distant places in search of the picturesque'. It was so popular

Spinning gallery, Cumbria

locally that he was once asked by a native whether he had written anything else. In its own class it still has no rival.

The basic merit of Wordsworth's Guide is that its aim was to seek out and define the innate character of the place – to describe accurately what is native to it. To Wordsworth this was intuitive. Hence the success. He saw the farmhouses, which in his day were clinging to mountainsides or huddled for shelter in disused quarries, as actually rising 'out of the naked rock – so little is there in them of formality – such is their wildness and beauty ...'. He went on to describe the larger farmhouses, with their wide gabled porches, which unlike the farm buildings were invariably limewashed (because lime provided a porous coating which allowed the rising damp to dry out), and the cottages, which had, instead of porches, 'two large slates over their thresholds', and gardens 'where yet may be seen specimens of those fantastic and quaint figures which our ancestors were fond of shaping out of yew-trees, holly or boxwood'. Happily, topiary work is as typical of farmhouse gardens in the Lake District today as it was when Wordsworth lived at 'the Mount'. According to a local mason who worked at Rydal in Wordsworth's time, the poet was passionately attached to regional idiosyncracies. He was, said the mason, 'a great un for chimleys. He had summat to say in the making of a deal of 'em hereabout.' There was 'most all the chimleys Rydal way built after his mind', and the mason remembered all the arguments that Wordsworth had with Dr Arnold of Rugby about the chimneys being built at Foxhow, Arnold's country home in the Lakes, which must have been a verbal contest between giants!

This particular interest is reflected in a detailed description in the *Guide*, concluding with the reflection: 'Nor will it be too fanciful or refined to remark, that there is a pleasant harmony between a tall chimney of this circular form, and the living column of smoke, ascending from it through the still air.'

The local farmhouse features most frequently pointed out to tourists doing the popular tour of the Lakes today are the open spinning galleries, built into the outer walls at first-floor level. Apparently most of them were added to existing buildings in the eighteenth century, judging by the turned wooden balusters of the one at Thorn House, Low Hartsop, and by the fact that they are usually, if not invariably, reached by external stairs. Most of them face north and seem to have been used for hanging out yarn to dry as well as for spinning. They may also have been used for storing fleeces. One of the best, in the sense of being one of the most typical, is at Yew Tree Farm, near Coniston. Never common in any part of England, they are not found in any other region today, and not more than fifteen have been recorded in Cumbria.

The slates that superseded thatch in the Lake District were local. The best were the green 'Borrowdale' and the 'Westmorland blue', both of which were heavy and rough-textured. Like Yorkshire and Cotswold roofing slabs, those in Cumbria were often pegged to the timbers with small bones from the shanks of sheep. The difference between the 'blue' and the 'green' arose from the former being Silurian, the latter volcanic. It was the masses of slate thrown up in volcanic convulsions that shaped Skiddaw. Vast quantities of 'Westmorland blues' from the quarries at Loughrigg, Elterwater and Tilberthwaite used to be brought down the mountain sides in 'trail barrows', which were sledges bearing wooden barrows or skips.

In the process of roofing, the slates were laid and pegged from the bottom, with those along the ridge placed alternately along each side and fixed with notches cut out of the corners to lock them together. These were called wrestlers, in allusion to the sport that has been popular in the Lake District as far back as records go and which, like horse-racing, may well have been introduced from Norway.

Another feature that seems to be Norwegian in origin is that other distinctively Cumbrian building the 'bank barn': a barn built against a natural embankment of the fell on a road terraced along a slope. These bank barns were built to provide access at two levels. Usually the whole of the upper floor was for storing hay, the lower was divided into three parts to provide for carts in the the middle, and animals at either end. Where that was the arrangement, the floor of the barn had flap doors through which hay could be dropped to the animals below. There is a bank barn at Low Hartsop, as mentioned, and also a corn-drying kiln, a feature that may have been common at one time but is now rare. These kilns were constructed on the same principle as bank barns but had grilles in the floor made of slates set edgeways to allow air to circulate and dry the damp grain.

Professor Adam Sedgwick, whose description of a Yorkshire farm kitchen was quoted in the previous chapter, contributed to more than one edition of Wordsworth's *Guide*, and his geological approach to the subject of Lake District scenery has been followed by several of the best writers on the Lakes. When we come to the social evolution of the region, the best clue, as in so many other places, is to be found in place-names. They are predominantly Norse and record the settlement of the region in the tenth century by men of hardy shepherd stock who landed in Morecambe Bay from Ireland, where they had established themselves in an earlier migration from Norway. From Ravenglass and Heysham they made their way up steep mountain passes, where sparkling water gushed through peat and bracken to tumble-down ravines, which they called gills, in whistling streams which they called becks.

Town End Bar, Troutbeck, Cumbria

Following the courses of these streams, they reached fertile land sloping down to lakes and tarns, and on these 'thwaites', as they called them, they built their homes.

From these group settlements, in accordance with the custom of their homeland, they drove their sheep and cattle each summer to mountain pastures, which were given Norse names, all showing how completely at home the shepherds felt among the Westmorland lakes and mountains.

Norse names are, in fact, found in all the upper reaches of the northern dales. There is a group of '-setts' in Upper Wensleydale: Appersett, Buttersett, Countersett and Marsett. But, for a systematic study of these early settlements and the kind of buildings that first stood on them, we need to go north into the mountain fastnesses where seasonal migrations continued into the seventeenth century. Fragments of buildings associated with this primitive form of local farming survive in broken walls that once enclosed folds and stackyards in which traces of plant life from kitchen gardens can still be found.

These relics of an abandoned way of life were examined by H.G. Ramm, R.W. McDowall and Eric Mercer for the Royal

Commission on Ancient Monuments (England).* The importance of their findings is not for archeologists only. They enable regional and family historians to identify sites of summer pastures used by families that have been farming in Cumbria for eight hundred years, and they help with the dating of farming innovations. As an example, describing an old bed of the Irthing river, well upstream, the name Noble Shields appear on old maps. A survey of the site identified seven huts – four of them on North Moor – of which few traces remain, suggesting that the huts were of turves, as one would expect them to be since there is no stone in the immediate vicinity. Such huts were usually rectangular in shape, measuring about ten feet by twenty, and few would have windows. Noble Shields is obviously the ancient shieling of the Noble family, now widely dispersed but still prolific, which had been closely associated for centuries with Bampton, west of the main road over Shap Fell. One member of the family wrote the history of Bampton, and Robert, my fifth-great-grandfather, carved the font in the parish church. Such is the continuity of family histories in these Cumbrian parishes. Most of the parish registers have been printed in the *Proceedings of the Cumberland and Westmorland Antiquarian Society*.

The wider significance of such sites is indicated in a Survey of 1604, which states: 'Each man knoweth his sheilinge steed, and they steylde together by surnames', a statement which indicates the existence of a clan spirit on the English side of the Border akin to that on the Scottish side. That this was so is borne out by North Country records of family feuds. Noble Shields is on a route much used by raiders from Nidderdale, and there appears to be evidence of the site being occupied by a small and poverty-stricken settlement of squatters, after the Noble family had abandoned their old summer pasture on developing all-the-year-round farming at Bampton when cattle rearing reduced dependence on sheep. No doubt this bit of family research could be repeated all along the Border.

That these primitive dwellings continued in use until the end of the seventeenth-century is confirmed by Celia Fiennes, who recorded that while riding through Westmorland in 1698 on her

Sheilings and Bastles, H.M.S.O., 1970

way to Scotland she found 'sad little huts made of dry walls, only stones piled together and roofs of the same slates, there seemed to be little or no tunnels for their chimneys and have no mortar or plaister within or without'. Nearly a hundred years later, James Clarke, is his *Survey of the Lakes* (1789) describes similar buildings, but we gather that they were then going out of use.

Wordsworth, tramping the fells at the end of the eighteenth century, saw them,

Clustered like stars some few, but singly most,
And lurking dimly in their shy retreats,
Or glancing at each other cheerful looks
Like separated stars with clouds between.

When these lines were written, most of the proud Westmorland 'statesmen' were crofters, with no more livestock grazing in the roughly walled enclosures alongside their cottages than a smallholder elsewhere would have. Their pride was in the Herdwicks grazing on the mountain behind them. In character and in the austere simplicity of their lives, they resembled the crofters in the Scottish Highlands. We get an idea of the houses they lived in by examining the cruck-built barns at Wall End, Great Langdale and Field Head Farm, Hawkshead.

Various theories about the origin of the Lake District Herdwicks have been advanced. Again, the best evidence is in the name. 'Herdwick' is Old English and means sheep-farm. As there are no fewer than twenty-five Herdwicks or Hardwicks in England, it seems remarkable that this particular breed should bear as its own distinctive name the general name of the farms that bred them. In the Middle Ages, when most of the flocks grazing the Yorkshire fells belonged to Fountains Abbey, the largest flocks in Westmorland and the parts of Lancashire that were in the Lake District ('Lancashire beyond the Sands') belonged to Furness Abbey. In the well-kept Furness records, Herdwicks are definitely sheepfarms, nor sheep. The transference must surely have come from the extraordinary attachment of this particular breed to its native heaf, Herdwicks, if allowed, will remain all their lives within a few yards of their place of birth. Although this traditional attachment is now being weakened by cross-breeding, they are still

141

exceptional in that they require only a minimal amount of care and are extraordinarily sensitive to changes in the weather.

The development of cattle farming to replace the dependence on sheep was slow in reaching proportions affecting farmhouse and farmstead lay-out. There were no entrepreneurs in Cumbria! Historically, it began when the Norse shepherd stock in the mountain-thwaites of the north-west linked up with the Anglo-Saxon and Danish settlers who had colonized the dales from the east. We find an instance of this in the Furness records, where there is an account of Furness Abbey buying most of Borrowdale as a sheepfarm in 1209, and in doing so becoming neighbours of Fountains, the owners of Watendlath and Langstrath. In their westward movement towards York, Norse names give place to Danish or Anglo-Saxon in the broad valleys first cultivated by the Anglo-Saxons, into which the Danes with their cattle had infiltrated earlier.

Valuable work has been done in recent years by Dr R.W. Brunskill, who has examined both Lake District farmhouses and contemporary records of their building – no doubt in estate papers deposited in county record offices. The distinctive plan is a local form of longhouse, divided into two parts by a screened passage running from front to back, with the house part, or fire-house, on one side and the 'down-house' on the other, behind a wattle-and-daub partition called the hallan. The name 'down-house' is significant because, as we have seen elsewhere, the shippons were built at the lower end to allow the slurry to seep away downhill.

The hallan passage, as in other longhouses, was generally used for storing sacks of fodder and hanging the carcases of pigs after slaughter. Horseshoes and other charms, such as crossed straws, were nailed over the door to ward off evil spirits.

The entrance to the fire-house from the hallan had a short spur, locally called a mell, on the house side to shield the hooded hearth from draughts. The outer wall of this short passage might be built out to provide space for a newel flight of stairs, built of slate, for access to the loft or upper rooms. An alternative was a similar flight of stairs at the back of the chimneybreast. Those who have examined the floors of these early farmhouses have found that they were of earth strongly reinforced with pebbles from the becks to assist drainage and reduce damp. Early this century they were invariably floored with blue slates.

At the far end of the fire-house a screened-off portion which had begun as a bed-chamber might be in use as a small private parlour. In the smallest houses a bed was built into a wall-recess of the living-kitchen and curtained off. These were called either cupboard beds or maternity beds, indicating their use for childbirth. Where the end of the fire-house had been brought into use as a parlour, the maternity bed might be build into the wall of that for greater privacy.

The main object of these wall recesses was to avoid draughts, and this applied equally to the ingle-nook, a term which suggests derivation from the Gaelic *aingeal*, fire, which, when taken in association with the term 'fire-house', brings out the full significance of the domestic quarters. The ingle was not the fireplace but the fire, which was the heart of the home to a degree we find difficult to appreciate. In seventeenth-century kitchens the ceiling of the open hearth was a foot or more higher than the rest of the room. This was to allow the smoke to collect into a large hood made of lath and plaster in the chimneybreast when there was insufficient air from below to drive it up the flue, or when there was a down-draught – a common nuisance in Lake District farmhouses and one from which the Wordsworths suffered. The usual remedy was to have two tilting slates propped against each other, firmly embedded in mortar, at the outlet. There was a small ingle-nook window called the 'fire-window' in the exterior wall at right-angles to the hearth. This was provided to admit light to the hearth and to act as a spy-hole when footsteps were heard approaching the house.

The fixed wooden bench, which stood on one side of the hearth, had a space underneath it where fuel for immediate use was usually stored. The long settle was much too heavy to move because the base of it served as a clothes chest, with the seat of the settle the lid of the chest. There was often a bible box under the fire-window, or on the shelf above it, with a lid which opened like a desk, so that the open bible could be laid on it when the head of the household read the 'daily portion' of Scripture at family prayers, a custom which continued into this century. There is a perfect reconstruction of a Westmorland farmhouse kitchen in the Wordsworth Museum at Grasmere.

Peat was stored in the down-house, where the household washing, brewing and pickling, as well as the daily dairy tasks, kept the women busy when not cooking, while the old ladies spent their time sewing, knitting or mending. From the rafters of the down-house hung meat salted in the brine-tub which every farmhouse had. The down-house was always cool, so when clothes had been washed and hung out to dry, they were brought into the kitchen to air on a long beam called the rannel-balk, which ran across the width of the hearth, with pot-hooks along the front of it for cooking-utensils to be hung on.

The custom of carving dates and initials on furniture is further evidence of the northerner's characteristic desire to leave his mark on the house he built or the object of his greatest pride. His home figured most strongly in this because it was the symbol of his freedom – the place where he was at all times 'his own man'. Lake District furniture tends to be too heavy to be suitable for less sturdily built houses, but the local style of chair, with the elaborately carved back, is still in great demand, as are such small pieces of kitchen equipment as cooking utensils and table dishes, which in the North were apparently made in wood longer than in the South, where pewter displaced wooden tableware in the seventeenth century. Porridge, for example, continued until recently to be served in wooden half-barrels called piggins.

Thanks to the generosity of Beatrix Potter, remembered locally as Mrs William Heelis, many unspoilt Lake District farmhouses are now the property of the National Trust. I remember her well as a little human bundle in a shawl, with Lancashire clogs on her feet, inspecting her sheep on the fell and in the distance looking almost indistinguishable from them. Although a wealthy woman, she would sometimes throw an old sack over her shoulders in bad weather to serve as a wrap. The favourite tale about her was of how, while climbing a rough mountain track in driving snow to see that her sheep were safe, she met an old tramp. 'Hard weather for the likes of thee and me,' muttered the tramp as he shuffled past. 'It is,' she replied without stopping. When she died in 1943, she was found to have left her home, Hill Top, Sawrey, to the National

Saltway Farm, near Calcot, Gloucestershire: in addition to the Roman
roads that cross the country, three old tracks occur in Gloucestershire; the
Welsh Way, the Calf Way, and the Salt Way. Saltway Farm stands beside
the latter and helps commemorate this past route from Droitwich. Note the
well-knit drystone wall in the garden

Hamlet of Duntisbourne Leer, Gloucestershire: with its large Leer Farm,
barn, and cottages all of honey-coloured stone Duntisbourne Leer epito-
mizes the popular idea of a charming Cotswold community

Aylworth Farm, Aylworth, Gloucestershire: an 18th-century house that contrasts rather starkly with more traditional forms of local architecture

Cleveland Farm, Longcot, Oxfordshire: the front of the house is slate-roofed and faced in chalkstone whilst the rear exhibits stone slates and rubble walls

Whitehouse Farm, near Witney, Oxfordshire: much harm has been done in recent years to the outward appearance of houses by the replacement of traditional windows. The visual charm of this particular farmhouse owes much to its windows and the use of light-coloured stone

Troy, near Somerton, Oxfordshire: the words troy or troy town used to mean a maze or labyrinth and there is an old turf maze in the attractive garden opposite this isolated

Ponden Hall, Scar Top, West Yorkshire: a sombre stone farmhouse of 17th-century date, it is reputed to be the source of inspiration for Thrushcross Grange in Emily Brontë's *Wuthering Heights*

Arncliffe, Littondale, North Yorkshire: a defensive village in which the farms cluster around a central green. The barn in the centre of the picture embodies a stone bearing the date 1677

Shillmoor, Upper Coquet Dale, Northumberland: although stone for the building of this Georgian farmhouse was most likely obtained locally, the roof slates would have had to be brought a considerable distance to such a remote spot. The windows are fitted internally with shutters to temper the worst of Cheviot winters

Hole Farm Bastle, near Bellingham, Northumberland: arguably the finest bastle still extant in Northumberland and remaining in use as an outbuilding of the present farm. The heavy stone steps appear to be of a later date than the original building which was intended for the protection of man and beast during the Border raids

Lemmington Branch, near Alnwick, Northumberland: has the deceptive appearance of a hillside fort. In fact it is a farmhouse screened by walls with mock battlements, arrow slits, and an exquisitely ogival-headed window

Blea Tarn Farm, Langdale Valley, Cumbria: with a deep Lakeland porch and the limewash traditionally favoured because it is porous and allows the walls to dry out more quickly when the sun breaks through

Dale Head Farm in the Duddon Valley: there are several Dale Head Farms in Cumbria, most of them more exposed than this one in Duddon. The local-style cylindrical chimney is just visible. The house is limewashed, but the porch is missing, suggesting a sheltered site

Trust, along with sixteen other farms – four thousand acres of land.

Of all the farmhouses owned by the National Trust in the Lake District, the finest is Townend, Troutbeck, acquired fully furnished in the 1940s along with eight hundred acres of land after being the home of the Browne family since it was built by George Browne in 1626. It still contains pieces of furniture made by him and his descendants from the seventeenth to the ninteenth century, carved with initials and dates. Townend has all the characteristics already enumerated, with the additional feature that the windows retain the original oak mullions, few of which are now left in other farmhouses, and some original panelling. Oak panelling was so common in the best farmhouses at the beginning of the present century that one wonders whether it was originally introduced for warmth and protection against damp. In some farmhouses the carving was linenfold, a design derived from the tapestry hangings in medieval castles and manor-houses. There have been alterations to the interior at Townend. The hallen is now a pantry and the down-house a kitchen, improvements which in most farmhouses of this character were carried out in the eighteenth and nineteenth centuries.

A major part of rural life still inadequately explored is the occupations and recreations of the winter months. In the Lake District, as in the Yorkshire Dales, when the day's work was done both men and women would sit together making peg rugs or patchwork quilts or knitting stockings by the light of flickering – we called them guttering – rushlights and candles. At the end of the eighteenth century 2,400 pairs of stockings were sold weekly on Kendal market and, according to Joseph Budworth,* six elderly knitters in Orton knitted seventy-six pairs of stockings monthly for a Kendal firm. To strengthen them for hard wear, the heels were smeared with pitch and then held over the ashes of a peat fire to set.

If life was hard, it was seldom dull. The planning of winter entertainments started at 'Back-end', the Lake District term for autumn. There were shepherds' neets (nights) and merry neets, at which the traditional fare was tatie-pot, which consisted of black puddings, Herdwick mutton, onions and potatoes, which together

*Joseph Budworth, *A Fortnight's Ramble in the Lakes*, 1792

made it a stronger mixture than Lancashire hotpot. Well-cooked mutton was quite as tender and more tasty than Common Market lamb. The modern prejudice against naming mature flesh is quite irrational – particularly in relation to chicken. This all-the-year-round nonsense has now been extended to turkey, and we have lost the joy of having each meat at its proper season, which was all part of the rhythm of life to countrymen two generations ago. To prepare for these winter social events, oats were dressed for meal in the kiln-croft in December and then taken to the 'bond-sucker' mill – a manorial hall to which the statesmen took their corn for grinding.

Generations before the advent of the Lake poets, there was a higher degree of literacy in the Lake District than in any other part of rural England. Westmorland was full of endowed grammer schools long before State education was introduced in 1833, and where there was no grammar school the parson conducted a village school in the parish church. So education in Cumbria, like so many other aspects of parish life, was comparable with that in the Scottish lowlands as described by Sir Walter Scott rather than that in any part of southern England. The strong Quaker tradition in Westmorland may have contributed to this. On the other hand, both may have been products of a more remote cause. At all events, it is reasonable to believe that, although there are fewer initialled and dated panels over farmhouse doors (not much local stone being suitable for carving), where they do occur the wife's initials are usually incorporated with her husband's.

For a description of a Lake District farmhouse at the end of the nineteenth century we have W.C. Collingwood's, in that other Lake District classic *The Lake Counties*:

> ... the low, rough-cast building with porch and penthouse (outside stair and gallery), dead-nailed door and massive thresh-wood, house-place with mullioned windows, and behind the rannal-balk a great open fire-spot where peats burned on the cobble-paved hearth, under the pot hanging from the ratten-crook; upstairs was the long loft, where the family slept unashamed as in the Icelandic *badsofa*. The exterior was charming, especially with big trees that overhung the mossy slates, and the massive chimneys, sometimes round and sometimes square. A bit of garden in which you saw the rock sticking

out, and a few clipped yews, and a humble imitation of the Elizabethan courtyard formed by the outbuildings, made the homestead a most picturesque feature, absolutely in harmony with the landscape.

The rugged drystone appearance is retained in the Lake District National Park today by keeping the mortar between the slate and rubble well back from the wall face whenever it becomes necessary to restore a building.

When we cross Stainmore out of Westmorland and Cumberland to enter County Durham, with its proud tradition of Prince-Bishops, and ducal Northumberland, we find ourselves in a dramatically different countryside. With more than eighty per cent of its population concentrated in the south-east corner, Northumberland has a vast landscape with grazing for more than a quarter of a million cattle. Only near the coast are climate and soil suitable for the arable farming introduced by Anglian settlers in the second half of the sixth century, of which traces can be seen as far inland as near Wooler. Again we look to place-names for clues to the character of early settlement and farming traditions. It seems surprising that only one village, Birling, near Warkworth, has the earliest Anglo-Saxon tribal ending, but the -inghams, from *ingas*, 'people of', are found up the valleys in places settled from the streams in such ancient centres as Ovingham, Bellingham, Chillingham and Ellingham, from which the numerous -hams, -tons, -wichs and -leys would be colonized. These Anglian settlements can still be identified independently of their names in compact villages strikingly different from the scattered farms and hamlets of Cumbria.

Danish names, which are so numerous along the east coast south of Northumberland, are entirely absent from Northumberland itself. Such Scandinavian names as there are appear to be Norse. So in Northumberland we are able to read on the landscape the difference between the tracks made by cattle and those made by sheep on the Lakeland fells. They are seen most distinctively leading to and from the fords where the cattle watered.

The main areas of sheep grazing country in Northumberland are in the west, which was formerly in the ownership of the bishopric of Durham and the monasteries associated with it. At the

Dissolution land-grabbers from Scotland gained possession of many of these old estates. The new owners did little for those who farmed the land and were hated by both the old aristocracy and the common people, to whom they were 'a spawn sprung from a dunghill birth'. These new owners became clan chieftains, and even today much of Northumberland remains a Scottish rather than an English scene. Thomas Pennant, the naturalist, touring the north in 1772, found Northumberland 'miserably depopulated, a few great farmhouses and hamlets, appear rarely scattered over vast tracts'.

These 'great farmhouses' were to become especially characteristic of Northumberland. Cobbett described them as being 'big enough for a gentleman to live in'. We return to them presently for the peles and bastles must set the scene. The name 'pele' is derived from the pale or palisade that enclosed the fortified farmstead. Most of the Northumberland peles were built in the fourteenth century, when private fortifications were permitted by law along the Scottish Border. They were of either two or three storeys, with the ground floor vaulted for strength, and either a straight or a newel staircase leading to the upper floor. Several of them are now incorporated in farmhouses and residences of large landowners, which may be called castles. Elsdon Pele, four miles east of Otterburn, is incorporated in a building that was formerly a fortified vicarage.

The dating of farm buildings in the north can seldom be precise since drystone walling continued in use until late. It can only be related safely to historical evidence of changing social conditions and farming methods, which again are more continuous in pastoral than in arable farming. The dominant consideration along the Border was security. From the peles evolved the bastles, which were more strongly fortified buildings in which the distinguishing feature is the accommodation of animals on the ground floor, the family on the upper floor or floors in the manner still found in the Alps but now found nowhere else in the British Isles. John Hodgson, the historian of Northumberland, describing one at Kirkwhelpington in 1827, comments that this would have been the usual type of Border farmhouse a century earlier.

The name seems to be derived from the French *bastille* and apparently appears only in dialect dictionaries of Northumberland.

In records of Cumberland estates there are references to stonehouses at the time when most crofters' farmhouses would be built largely of turf and drystone walling in shale or slate. These stonehouses must have been what in Northumberland were called bastles. Both were built of large blocks of irregularly shaped stone, infilled with stone chippings and mortar. The walls of both were four feet thick at ground-floor level, with only narrow slits for ventilation. The doorway was at one of the gable ends and so narrow that oxen of the girth used in the southern counties could not have squeezed through them. They were probably adequate for sheep and a few cattle kept by hill farmers at the time they were built, which would be at any date between 1540 and the middle of the seventeenth century. Their advantage as farmhouses would be that the animals on the ground floor would provide an effective form of central heating for the family above!

The upper floors of surviving bastles and stonehouses are now reached by stone steps, but as these are not bonded into the wall, we may assume they replaced ladders which could be drawn up when cattle-thieving families like the Armstrongs were on the prowl and the Robsons and Reeds had gone out to meet them, leaving their families and their stock secure in their bastles. All these heavily fortified buildings are within about twenty miles of the Border. The one or two outside this band are said to be of doubtful authenticity. The district most thickly strewn with bastles was on the banks of the Warks burn, a tributary of the North Tyne, where large herds of cattle were fattened.

Apart from the regular forayes, the vast estates of Border landowners like the Nevilles, the Percies and the Dacres were always subject to political upheavals and the fortunes of war, which might bring them into the stagnation of royal hands for periods of up to twenty years. The insecurity of the region was such that a Survey of 1541 stated that anyone who would settle on land in Kidland could live rent free. Farm names like Unthank – which means 'occupied without thanks' or pay – indicate how much land there was in the north of England that was anyone's for the taking.

The most interesting of the surviving bastles is Housesteads at Bardon Mill, where the Roman fort has a bastle built east of the south gateway of the outer wall. A drying-kiln has been built into the Roman guardroom, and Roman material has been used throughout the later buildings. The whole scene is ready-made for a thrilling Border romance. It was probably the home of Hugh Nixon, a seventeenth-century reiver and receiver of stolen goods, and before that had been the headquarters of the Armstrongs, a family that could have provided Blackmore with as good, if not better, material than the Doones supplied in Devon – and the Doones, remember, came from Scotland.

The Act of Union between England and Scotland did not bring the raids to an end, so it was not until well into the eighteenth century that there was any agricultural development to speak of in Northumberland. Eventually, however, the reivers north of the Border settled down to more peaceful pursuits, and the square Georgian and early Victorian farmhouses that are such a feature of the Percy estates bear witness to the prosperous cattle-fattening days associated with cattle-droving and the great fairs of eastern England.

10. *The Agrarian Revolution*

Cottage garden, Devon

So long as the sovereign continued to be the source of political power, it was inevitable that with the advent of a new reigning House every ambitious landowner would be anxious to appear in the guise most favourable to himself and most flattering to the sovereign. The surest way of doing this was by building himself a splendid new mansion and housing his tenant-farmers in a manner calculated to reflect prosperity. This largely explains the building boom of 1580 to 1650 which has been the subject of much of this book. Elizabeth I was responsible for a great deal of it in her Progresses through the realm, which impoverished some of her most ambitious subjects. James I had no illusions about what was happening. When he visited Audley End in Essex, he remarked: 'By my troth, mon, it is too much for a king, but may do for a Lord High Treasurer.'

The accession of the Georges prompted three of the Whig dukes,

151

Devonshire, Portland and Bedford, to present themselves impressively, which, when the Industrial Revolution got under way, they were able to do with wealth derived from mineral-bearing land and commercial interests in the new towns of the Midlands, as well as in London itself. Coal was the main source of this new wealth.

The great landowners of the north followed suit. A few gambled or drank away their gains, but most of them were hard-headed and shrewd. In Yorkshire the most outstanding of these in the middle years of the eighteenth century was Henry Lascelles of Northallerton, who from wealth acquired as a West India sugar merchant bought the village of Harewood and the hamlet of Stank, together with the ruins of Harewood Castle and in 1739 the Jacobean house at Gawthorpe. His son, the first Lord Harewood, and his successor, Edward, first Earl of Harewood, consolidated the estates and from 1753 onwards rebuilt practically every property on them on a scale hitherto unattempted in the North. Harewood village was rebuilt entirely to a design by Carr of York, who received £60 a year from Edwin Lascelles as official surveyor to the estate, an office he also held at Wentworth Woodhouse.

Lofthouse Farm, opposite the original main gate to Harewood House, may safely be attributed to him. Although an independent architect of stature in his own right, Carr could not have failed to be influenced by the work of Daniel Garrett, who died in 1753, the year before the replanning of the Harewood estate started in earnest. Garrett's *Designs and Estimates of Farm-Houses etc. for the County of York, Northumberland, Cumberland, Westmorland and the Bishopric of Durham* had been published in 1747 as the first English architectural work entirely devoted to farm designs. It influenced the work of architects engaged to rebuild farmhouses in the old West Riding of Yorkshire at Aldwarke, Allerton, Bretton, Campsall, Carlton, Huthwaite, Nostell, Ornhams, Plompton, Sandbeck, Wighill and Wentworth Woodhouse.

The influence continued northward through the vast estates of the East and North Ridings, and into the Percy estates in Northumberland. In Westmorland the village of Lowther was rebuilt in the 1760s by Sir James Lowther to a design by the Adam brothers, setting a new standard in a region that had been at least a hundred years behind Yorkshire in its local styles. There the changes were resisted by the 'statesmen', with their long memories of 'customary leases', in which hereditary privileges of tenancy were enjoyed in return for the tenants' undertaking to be ready at their own cost to go in defence of the Border whenever the Scots invaded. As the two thrones had been united, Border service had become an anachronism, and the Lowthers led a movement to grant new leases at double the existing rents in recognition of release from military commitments. The tenants resisted. Apart from the monetary considerations, fighting the marauding Scots was part of the local way of life. And what right had 'the wicked Lord Lowther' to manipulate to his own advantage their ancient tenures? Seventy-three years after the accession of James I, when Roger North looked into the rights and wrongs of the disputes, he shrewdly observed that, in any disputes coming before the courts, 'the verdicts would always be sure to be in favour of the tenants, because country juries, almost to a man, were drawn from them.'

The landowners of Northumberland were better placed to gain co-operation because they had a depressed, not a proud, tenancy to deal with, and Arthur Young in 1768 found that, 'Farms become large on entering Northumberland, after the small ones of Yorkshire and Durham.' His reference to Yorkshire was to the dales in the extreme north and, as he couples it with Durham, means that he had Teesdale and perhaps Swaledale in mind. But everywhere there was an inbred prejudice against estate planning and the divisive power of wealth brought about by external political and economic forces. Equally there was a gut reaction against the size of the houses being built, because of their ostentatious grandeur and of all it symbolized. They were un-English and alien to the traditional rural way of life in every part of the Kingdom. Alexander Pope wrote of them:

Thanks Sir, I cried, 'tis very fine,
But where d'ye sleep, or where d'ye dine?
I find by all you have been telling
That 'tis a house, but not a dwelling.

Vanbrugh (whose palatial mansions inspired the Reverend Abel Evans to suggest that when he died a suitable epitaph for him would be:

Lie heavy on him earth, for he
Laid many a heavy load on thee)

himself wrote: 'One may find a great deal of Pleasure in building a
Palace for another; when one should find very little in living in't
ones Self.'

Cobbett's contempt for the new generation of farmers who
emulated the landowners in the new style of living reached its peak
as he stood in front of a Surrey farmhouse and cursed it as a Quaker
might fulminate against a church steeple. He did not deny that
there had been what we now call a rise in the standard of living. He
acknowledged it. But to the Old Testament prophet in him it all
amounted to shameless worship of the Golden Calf. He scorned the
petty pretence of farmers who were abandoning the stout oak they
had inherited from their forebears – both literally and figuratively
– and refurnishing their houses with mahogany imported from
America. He denounced the family move out of the kitchen into the
'parlour', a room which to him was a social abomination in a
farmhouse.

Describing the farmhouse that incurred his wrath, he wrote:
'One end of this once plain and substantial house has been moulded
into a parlour; and there was the mahogany table, and the fine
chairs, and the fine glass, and all as bare-faced upstart as any
stock-jobber in the kingdom can boast of. This "squire"
Charrington's father used, I dare say, to sit at the head of the oak
table along with his men, say grace to them, and cut up the meat
and the pudding. He might take a cup of strong beer to himself,
when they had none; but that was pretty nearly all the difference in
their manner of living, so they all lived well.' Now, he went on, the
new squire had 'wine decanters and wine glasses and a dinner set,
and a breakfast set, and desert knives', all to Cobbett implying
'carryings on and consumption that must of necessity have greatly
robbed the long table if it had remained fully tenanted'.

To understand the emotional reaction to the revolution which
disrupted the countryside as well as the towns in the
eighteenth and nineteenth centuries, one has to appreciate the way
the social structure of England, hitherto predominantly rural, had
been held together by the sharing of common interests in crops,

livestock, field sports and pastimes on village greens. Interest in these had overridden all differences in class or wealth. The exploitation of mineral deposits in the Midlands and the North, and progressive urbanization in the South as landowners acquired City interests, broke up these daily links between rich and poor as estates were enlarged and agents employed to deal with tenancy problems.

The movement that provoked the longest and bitterest controversy was the great Enclosure drive, in which Cobbett and a score of lesser writers fulminated against 'the infernal system of Pitt and his followers', which they alleged was impoverishing the countryside by amalgamating holdings and turning small farmers into hired hands. According to Cobbett, in the region around Windsor three out of every four farmhouses had been pulled down, while in Hampshire the farm buildings were 'dropping down bit by bit'.

There had been similar tirades in Tudor times, when Bishop Latimer declared that sheep were 'devouring men' as vast areas of common fields, which had given employment to entire villages, were being sacrificed for easy profit to be derived from wool on the backs of flocks of sheep which one man with a dog could herd.

The dispute in Cobbett's day was more complex. Sheep had become valuable as producers of mutton as well as wool, cattle as producers of beef as well as milk, and to develop these new sources of wealth farming had become more scientific, which meant that more capital had to be injected into it than the small farmer could raise. The process has continued at an accelerating rate into our own day. The 1851 census showed that there were then 1,788,000 farm workers in England. What, we may wonder, would Cobbett, who died in 1835, have said about the situation at the present time, with not more than 200,000 left on the land, and the number continuing to fall? During a recent visit to the West of England, while touring the countryside for the purpose of this book, I was greeted by a fine old countryman who had retired from senior employment on one of the largest farms in north Essex. He told me that he could no longer bear to go back to the place that had been his pride for fifty years. When he started work on the same farm as a youth, there were thirty men employed on it; now there were

155

only two. 'There may be more profit from farming now than there was then,' he commented, 'but it is no longer a satisfing way of life, and a good one!'

As in all revolutionary changes, there were both gainers and losers in the eighteenth century, and most generalizations about them are blinkered. Inevitably, it was the weakest who went to the wall. So on the one hand we have Arthur Young's picture of the small farmer who by a narrow margin had managed to survive the enclosure of his land as an independent tenant. 'He works harder,' Young wrote, 'and fares harder than the common labourer; and yet with all this labour and all his fatiguing incessant exertions, seldom can he at all improve his condition or even with any degree of regularity pay his rent and preserve his present situation. He is confined to perpetual drudgery.' On the other hand W.H. Curtler wrote: 'Before enclosure the farmer entertained his friends with bacon fed by himself, washed down with ale brewed from his own malt, in a brown jug, or a glass if he were extravagant. He wore a coat of woollen stuff, the growth of his own flock, spun by his wife and daughters, his stockings came from the same quarter, so did the clothes of his family'.*

After the Napoleonic Wars, and with the advantages resulting from the increased yield of enclosed land properly manured, and the inflated prices that organized agriculture could command, the average farmer's style of living did rise to that which the squire had enjoyed earlier. In Cobbett's admittedly over-coloured account, he now had 'a fox-hunting horse; polished boots; a spanking trot to market; a "get out of the way or by G-d I'll ride over you" to every poor devil upon the road; wine at dinner; a servant (and sometimes in livery) to wait at his table; a painted lady for a wife; sons aping the young squires and lords; a house crammed up with sofas, pianos and all sorts of fooleries'.

However, in all these changes, with gains and losses unevenly divided, there was one part of England where the farmer's lot was so much 'all gain' that even Cobbett could not fault it. This was on the Holkham estate in Norfolk, which, when the great 'Coke of Norfolk' inherited it at the age of twenty-four in 1776, already

*Curtler, W.H.H., A Short History of English Agriculture, Oxford, 1909

extended over 43,000 acres. But so much of it was then sandy waste that the idea of raising crops on it was ridiculed. Despite this, Coke employed men on his home estate so successfully that he increased the population from two hundred in 1776 to eleven thousand by 1818, and his rental income rose during those years from £2,200 a year to £20,000. Visiting the estate in 1822, the old curmudgeon wrote: 'Here at Holt as everywhere else, I hear every creature speak loudly in praise of Coke. It is well known to my readers that I think nothing of him as a *public* man ... but it would be base in me not to say that I hear from men of all parties, and sensible men too, expressions made use of towards him that affectionate children use towards the best of parents. I have not met a single exception.'

Model cottages for estate hands as well as commodious farmhouses for tenant farmers, enormous barns of white brick, and houses for stock were built. In middle age Coke himself declared: 'It has been objected against me that my tenants live too much like gentlemen, driving their own curricles, perhaps, and drinking their port every day. I am proud to have such a tenantry, and heartily wish that instead of drinking their port they could afford to drink their claret and champagne every day.' Other Norfolk farmer-landowners followed his lead. One, Henry Overman of Weasenham, planned on such a scale that Young commented that, if the rage for building did not cease, half the land would be covered with barns to hold the corn for the other half.* The conversion of sandy wastes into fertile acres had been achieved by irrigation and manure – especially the latter from cattle fed on root crops, giving rise to the Norfolk proverb: 'Muck is the mother of money.' The Duke of Bedford followed the Norfolk lead on his estates at Woburn, and Lord Egremont at Petworth in Sussex. There was no criticism whatever from the old nobility when in 1837 Thomas Coke of Holkham was created Earl of Leicester.

Like 'His Honour' Sir Thomas Acland in the West of England, Coke encouraged his tenants to regard the land they rented as their best investment by granting twenty-one year leases, the terms of which became models for progressive landowners throughout England. Every county had them, the wealthiest landowners

---

*Young, *A Week in Norfolk* (Oct. 1792) Annals of Agriculture., XIX, p. 451

competing with each other in building model villages and farmhouses. Cobbett, however, remained unconvinced to the end of his life that the changes in the status of the farmer were for better and, although his attacks on the new system were biassed, there was usually at least a grain of truth in what he said – often more than a grain. On the new custom of building cottages for farm workers instead of accommodating most of them with the farmer's own family in the farmhouse, he asked rhetorically, 'Why do not farmers now feed and lodge their work-people, as they did formerly?' and provided his own answer: 'Because they cannot keep them upon so little as they give them in wages.' There was also the loss of those evening sessions round the kitchen fire in which master and men would exchange views on the day's labour and plan the course for the morrow.

But the changes were not all reflections of personal pride on the farmer's part. In the countryside best known to Cobbett, that of the southern downs, better farmhouses were being built that had nothing to do with social ambition. Largely through the better use of manure, cultivated land was being extended up the foothills of the downs providing pastures on which bullocks could be fattened. This was done by enclosing folds for cattle, in which manure could be accumulated for spreading on the land. Much of Salisbury Plain was reclaimed in this way, and the process developed by the building of outlying barns in which hay could be stored to feed the cattle with in winter. In some places herdsmen's cottages, which eventually became small farmhouses, were built nearby, giving the completed groups the appearance of independent smallholdings.

In the hill country of the South-West and North-West of England eighteenth- and nineteenth-century rebuilding was minimal. The stone farmhouses built in the seventeenth-century building boom continued to serve, with such improvements as have already been discussed in the chapter on the South-West under such benevolent and enlightened landowners as the Aclands and Welds. The same may be said of much of the North of England. In the Yorkshire dales life continued, as it does to this day, to maintain a quiet dignity. The people knew their own weather and the potentialities of the land they tilled. Every hill farmer has tales about men 'with more money than sense' who started experimenting with lowland methods for which the region was unsuitable and who went bankrupt within ten years. The dependence is still on sheep, and apparently today a hill farmer needs five hundred breeding ewes to maintain what an East Anglian farmer would regard as a reasonable standard of living.

There was, however, one feature in the northern climate that proved favourable. The bracing air and sweet grass, when limed and manured, was found to be ideal for improving stock-breeding. The fine, well-proportioned farmhouses round Skipton in Craven, especially those under Ingleborough, Pennyghent and Whernside, are as clearly the creations of 'improving landlords' as those found in the planned landscapes of the Peak in Derbyshire, the Harewood estates of north Yorkshire and the Percy estates of Northumberland. Scientific stock-breeding has a long history in the north. It was started by the Cistercians and continued after the Dissolution until eventually it found expression in county shows. As elsewhere, the pride of the landowners filtered through to the tenant farmers, who were well supported by their wives, whose role in farm life continues to expand, rather than contract, as a result of so much of their traditional dairy work being done commercially. They compete on equal terms with men in agricultural shows and in actual showmanship have nothing to learn from them. Their enrichment of the domestic side of farm life finds expression in every meeting of that great rural institution, the Women's Institutes.

Even when the farmer's wife and her maidservants were kept busy from dawn to dusk indoors, the farmyard fowls were their especial care, and early this century it was customary for money collected from the sale of eggs to be kept by them as 'pin-money': money saved or earned by the women for personal expenditure. But they were also the creators of the typical farmhouse and cottage gardens so charmingly described by Mary Mitford in *Our Village*, with in spring 'their gay bunches of polyanthuses and crocuses, their wallflowers, sending sweet odours through the narrow casement'. In summer there were, and still are, hollyhocks, roses and honeysuckle, followed by dahlias, chrysanthemums and Christmas roses.

Larkspur, white lilac and laburnum were there in Shakespeare's

159

time. Beans, carrots, cabbages, peas, parsnips, onions and salad herbs were brought in from the garden daily when in season but were formerly put into what we call 'the stock pot' instead of being served from separate dishes with the main course. Simples – herbaceous plants with medicinal properties – were grown for household remedies when there was no National Health Service. Baring-Gould loved to tell the story of a conversation he had with a parishioner while rector of East Mersea in Essex. On asking how far the old man had to go to see the nearest doctor, he received the reply. 'Maybe ten miles, sir. But us don't bother with 'ee. Thank God most on us dies natural deaths in these parts.' No doubt he had his own remedies. In the sixteenth century William Harrison, while parson of Radwinter in Essex, grew 'very near three hundred' different simples in his garden.

Orchard trees, apart from apples and natives such as damsons, were slower in being generally adopted because there was a curious prejudice against fruit. It was feared that it might be affected by the insects that lighted on the trees at blossom time, and the grubs that might be found in decayed fruit. Pepys in 1661 wrote in his Dairy: 'in the afternoon had notice that my Lord Hinchinbrooke is fallen ill, which I fear is with the fruit that I did give them on Saturday last at my house; so in the evening I went thither and there found him very ill, and in great fear of smallpox'.

The importation of most of the fruit and garden shrubs that are not natives developed in Elizabethan times from plants brought in from the Indies, Canary Isles and other parts of the world by the Merchant Adventurers, so did not reach gardens in the Midlands and North to any great extent until much later. Since most of the farms in the Midlands have houses dating only from the Enclosure awards of 1760-1820, farmhouse gardens tend to be less interesting from the historical point of view than those in the South-West and the South-East. Their interest is in the lay-out of the villages in relation to estate planning, particularly in the building of Georgian farmhouses and uniform cottages for farm-workers. Lord Harcourt's eighteenth-century rebuilding of Nuneham Courtenay with semi-detached cottages lining the village street is an outstanding example.

Undoubtedly the Surveys made by Arthur Young in the 1770s

and William Marshall later did much to encourage the movement. Between 1787 and 1798 the Board of Agriculture published twelve volumes of Reports under a lengthy title that may be shortened to *General Survey of the Rural Economy of England*. George III experimented in cattle breeding on the royal farm at Windsor, and as 'Ralph Robinson' contributed personally to the *Annals of Agriculture*. This 'golden Age' extended into the reign of Victoria, who gave her patronage to the Royal Agricultural Society, founded in 1838 and incorporated by Royal Charter in 1840. The agricultural shows organized by the society were the social events of the farming year. The Prince Consort interested himself in experimenting with designs for dairies at Windsor, Osborne and the estate of the Prince of Wales, afterwards Edward VII, at Sandringham. The old dairy at Frogmore was rebuilt with floors and walls covered with glazed tiles, tables of marble, shelves of slate, and windows double-glazed. Fountains played perpetually in them to keep down the temperature.

Now, in the last quarter of the twentieth century, we are witnessing another agrarian revolution. The social fabric of the nation is not threatened by it. Royal patronage remains strong, and the Prince of Wales is closely identifying himself with the interests of his tenants in both the Duchy of Cornwall and the Principality of Wales. The interest in agricultural shows is as great as ever. At the same time we have our present-day Cobbetts, and the striking of a balance between urban and rural attitudes towards farming has been complicated by large estates passing in increasing numbers out of private into institutional ownership. The case for this is strong in economic terms, but it is difficult to believe that these new owners, however well disposed they may be, can have the attitude of stewardship in the control of their estates that was symbolized at Holkham under the first commoner to be raised to the peerage by Queen Victoria. At major estate functions and festive occasions we may be confident that the Loyal Toast will continue to be honoured, but will it be followed by the second Holkham toast: 'Live and Let Live'?

Appendix

A selection of museums and buildings that may be visited:
(times of opening should be ascertained before visiting; farmhouses
not listed below are in the main private property and should be
respected as such)

National Trust properties in all parts of England

South-West England
Lanreath Mill and Museum, near Looe, Cornwall
Somerset Rural Life Museum, Glastonbury

South-East England
Weald and Downland Open Air Museum, Singleton, near
    Chichester
Wye College Agricultural Mmuseum, Brook, near Ashford

Essex and East Anglia
Upminster Tithe Barn Agricultural and Folk Museum
Museum of East Anglian Life, Abbot's Hall, Stowmarket
Easton Park Farm, Easton, Woodbridge
Wandlebury Ring, near Cambridge

The Cotswolds
Smerrill Farm Museum, Kemble, near Cirencester
Oxfordshire County Museum, Manor Farm, Cogges, Witney
Tithe barns in many National Trust Properties: Ashleworth,
    Bredon, Great Coxwell etc.

West Midlands
Avoncroft Museum of Buildings, near Bromsgrove

163

Hereford and Worcester County Museum, Hartlebury Castle, Hartlebury

Mary Arden's House, Wilmcote, near Stratford-on-Avon

Home Farm, Acton Scott, near Church Stretton (Shropshire County Museum)

Museum of Staffordshire Life, Shugborough Hall, Great Haywood

Berkshire
Museum of Agricultural Life, University of Reading

West Yorkshire
East Riddlesden Hall, near Keighley
Pennine Folk Museum, Ripponden
West Yorkshire Folk Museum, Shibden Hall, Halifax

Durham
North of England Open Air Museum, Beamish Hall, Stanley

Lake District
National Trust properties

Select Bibliography

Agriculture, Board of, *General View of the Agriculture of* ... (Series) 1793-1815.

Atkinson, T.D., *Local Style in English Architecture* (Batsford, 1947)

Balchin, W.G.V., *Cornwall* (The Making of the English Landscape Series, 1954)

Barley, M.W., *The English Farmhouse and Cottage* (Routledge and Kegan Paul, 1961)

Beastall, T.H., *The Agricultural Revolution in Lincolnshire* (Lincs. Loc. Hist. Soc., 1979)

Beatson, R., *On Farm Buildings* (1796)

Beresford, M.W., *The Lost Villages of England* (Lutterworth Press, 1954)

Bowen, H.C., *Ancient Fields* (British Association for the Advancement of Science, 1961)

Braun, Hugh, *Old English Houses* (Faber and Faber, 1962)

Briggs, Martin S., *The English Farmhouse* (Batsford, 1963)

Brill, Edith, *Life and Tradition in the Cotswolds* (Dent, 1973)

Brunskill, J., *Vernacular Architecture of the Lake Counties* (Faber, 1978)

Brunskill, R.W., *Illustrated Handbook of Vernacular Architecture* (Faber, 1978)

Budworth, Joseph, *A Fortnight's Ramble in the Lakes* (1792)

Caird, James, *English Agriculture, 1850-51* (1852)

Cambridge Agrarian History, Vol. IV and VIII (Camb. Univ. Press, 1967, 1978)

Carew, Richard, *Survey of Cornwall* (1602)

Chambers, J.D., and Mingay, G.E., *The Agricultural Revolution 1750-1880* (Batsford, 1966)

Clarke, James, *Survey of the Lakes* (1789)

Clifton-Taylor, A.,*The Pattern of English Building* (Faber, 1972)

Cobbett, William, *Rural Rides* (1830)

Collingwood, W.G., *The Lake Counties* (Dent, 1902, 1949 reprint)

Curtler, W.H.R., *A Short History of English Architecture* (Oxford, 1909)

Curtler, W.H.R., *The Enclosure and Redistribution of Our Land* (Oxford, 1920)

Darley, Gillian, *The Farm* (The National Trust, Weidenfeld and Nicolson, 1981)

Denton, J.B., *The Farm Homesteads of England* (1863)

165

Derrick, Freda, *Cotswold Stone* (Chapman and Hall, 1948)

Eliot, George, novels.

Ernle, Lord (R.E. Prothero), *English Farming Past and Present* (Heinemann, 1961)

Fox, Sir Cyril, and Lord Raglan, *Monmouthshire Houses*, three vols (National Museum of Wales, 1951-54)

Garrett, Daniel, *Designs and Estimates of Farmhouses* (1747)

Gonner, E.C.K., *Common Land and Inclosure* (Macmillan, 1912)

Gotch, J.A., *The Growth of the English House* (Batsford, Revised Edn. 1928)

Haggard, Sir Rider, *Rural England* (1902)

Hardy Thomas, novels and poems.

Harris, Alan, *The Rural Landscape of the East Riding of Yorkshire, 1700-1850* (Oxford, 1961)

Harrison, William, *Description of England* (first published in Holinshed's *Chronicle*, 1577)

Hartley, Dorothy, *The Land of England* (Macdonald, 1979)

Hartley, Marie, and Ingleby, Joan, *Life and Traditions in the Yorkshire Dales* (Dent, 1972)

Harvey, N., *History of Farm Buildings in England and Wales* (David and Charles, 1979)

Hodgson, John, *History of Northumberland* (1827)

Hoskins, W.G., *The Making of the English Landscape* (Hodder and Stoughton, 1955, Penguin Books, 1970)
Editor of the Series of that name and author of the *Leicestershire* volume.

Hoskins, W.G., *Provincial England* (Macmillan, 1963, Chap. 7)

Hoskins, W.G., 'Some Old Devon Bartons' (*Country Life*, 22 Sep. 1950)

Howitt, William, *The Rural Life of England* (1840)

Kerr, Barbara, *Bound to the Soil* (John Baker, 1968)

Kerr, Barbara, 'The Dorset Agricultural Labourer, 1750-1850', Dor. Nat. Hist. and Arch. Soc. Proc., 1962.

Lambarde, William, *The Perambulation of Kent* (first printed in 1574)

Loudon, John Claudius, *Encyclopaedia of Cottage, Farm, and Villa Architecture* (1836)

Markham, Gervase, *The English Husbandman* (1613)

Marshall, William, *Rural Economy of Norfolk, 1787; Yorkshire, 1788; Gloucestershire, 1789; The Midland Counties*, 1790

Mercer, Eric, *English Vernacular Houses* (H.M.S.O., 1975)

Mercer Eric, with Ramm, H.G., and McDowall, R., *Shielings and Bastles* (H.M.S.O., 1970)

Morris, Christopher, (ed.) *The Journals of Celia Fiennes* (Cresset Press, 1947)

National Trust Guides and publications.

Orwin, C.S., *A History of English Farming* (Nelson, 1949)

Page, William, 'The Origins and Forms of Hertfordshire Towns and Villages', *Archaeologia* LXIX, 1917-18.

Palmer, J.H., *Historic Farmhouses in and Around Westmorland, Westmorland Gazette*, revised edn. 1952)

Plaw, J., *Ferme Ornée* (1795)

Raistrick, A., *The Story of the Pennine Walls* (The Dalesman Pub. Co., Clapham, Yorks, 1952)

Read, Sir Herbert, *Annals of Innocence and Experience* (1940)

Robinson, P.F., *Rural Architecture* (1823)

Robinson, P.F., *Designs of Farm Buildings* (1830)

Rowley, Trevor, *Shropshire* (The Making of the English Landscape Series, from 1954)

Seebohm, F., *The English Village Community* (Camb. Univ. Press, 1926 edn.)

Stamp, L. Dudley, *Britain's Structure and Scenery* (Collins, 1968)

Thirsk, Joan, (ed.), *The Agrarian History of England, 1500-1640* (Routledge and Kegan Paul, 1967)

Trent, Christopher, *The Changing Face of England* (Phoenix House, 1956)

Victoria County History of England, especially the Essex volumes.

Webb, Mary, Shropshire novels, especially *Precious Bane*

Weller, J., *History of the Farmstead* (Faber, 1982)

Whitaker, T.D., *History of Craven* (1805)

Williams-Ellis, Clough, and Eastwick-Field, John and Elizabeth, 'Building in Cob, Pisé, and Stabilised Earth' (*Country Life*, 1947)

Wordsworth, William, *Guide to the Lakes* (fifth edn. 1835; Oxford University Press, edited by Ernest de Selincourt, 1977)

Young, Arthur, Board of Agriculture Reports (1793-1815)

Index